Democracy and Social Change in South Korea

Democracy and Social Change in South Korea

Jong Bin Yoon & Soo Hyun Jung et al.

Edited by Center for Future Policy Studies

PURUNGIL BOOKS

This book was written for faculty and students who are interested in democracy and political change in South Korea. To do so, the chapters of the book are organized into five Parts.

In Part I, current political challenges for Korean democracy are examined. Jong Bin Yoon explains the causes of the crisis of Korean representative democracy. Jeeyoung Park investigates the increasing political polarization since the impeachment of president Park Geun-hye. Dong-Joon Jung addresses several ways to resolve these problems: introduction of more direct democratic mechanisms, the protection of substantive democratic values through judicial review, and, more profoundly, inculcating democratic norms in the minds of both elites and ordinary citizens.

Part II examines various issues of social conflict and inequality in Korea. Jungsub Shin explains growing economic inequality since the 1990 financial crisis and its effects on class politics. Hoiok Jeong investigates social diversity change due to the influx of immigrants and Koreans' negative attitudes toward immigrants. Euisuok Han examines generational conflicts in Korean politics and economy. His conclusion is that that generational conflicts intensified in politics during the 2000s and in the economic sphere during 2010s, reflecting democratization, globalization and neo-liberalization.

Part III looks at social inclusion and political tolerance. Sung-jin Yoo investigates public attitudes toward three social minorities in Korea: immigrant workers, members of the LGBT community, and North Korean refugees. His analysis shows that the Korean public has lower level of political tolerance when compared to Western countries, and public attitudes toward LGBT people as a group are saliently negative even today. Jinju Kim investigates examine the extent of social inclusion and political tolerance that Koreans hold towards the multicultural population. As a result, she suggests that it is necessary to seek activities that enable multicultural people and Koreans to form deep relationships, and to promote Koreans' awareness of toward multicultural people.

In Part IV, the development of information technology and political communication in Korea is examined. Hana Kim analyzes political content on YouTube and explains how Korean politicians communicate with and persuade voters using various mass media based on the Sender-Message-Channel-Receiver (SMCR) model of communication. Shin-Il Moon provides an informative context to help readers understand the relationship between ICT development and political communication. Kitae Kim examines various issues of machine lerarning algorithms from the perspective of user protection (e.g., the creation of filter bubbles in online communities, algorithmic bias and unfairness, and concerns about privacy infringement), illustrates some substantive cases where they can arise, and discusses the necessary components of an algorithmic governance system to prepare for the 4th industrial revolution era.

The final Part of the book involves party politics and public deliberation in Korea. Kyungmee Park looks at splits and mergers of the Korean political parties since the 1987 democratization by analyzing the relationship between parties and citizens historically, and then discusses membership of the Korean parties focusing on how citizens engage in and with parties. Soo Hyun Jung reviews the background, processes, and outcomes of several deliberative forums that were conducted in South Korea, and points out existing problems in public deliberation.

We have received much help along the way. This project's main source of financial assistance is the Ministry of Education of the Republic of Korea and the National Research Foundation of Korea (NRF-2019S1A3A2098969). We deeply appreciate the NRF. Special thanks go to David J. Hendry from the London School of Economics and Political Science and Sojeong Kim for their help and support. We continue to enjoy our relationship with Purungil Books. Finally, we thank our families for their assistance and patience.

Jong Bin Yoon
Soo Hyun Jung

Contents

Part I

Political Challenge for Korean Democracy

01

The Nature of Representative Democracy in South Korea

Jong Bin Yoon
Myongji University

South Korea experienced dramatic political and social changes both before and after the 1987 democratic movement. On the social side, Korea entered into the Aging Society combined with a record low birth rate. On the political side, as shown by the candlelight vigils in 2008 and 2016, the public desire for political participation has escalated. It is commonly believed that the tendency toward strong street demonstrations in Korea is caused by a systemic lack of political responsiveness. Further, the extraordinary impeachment of the President Park could be a noteworthy example of the crisis of representative democracy.

The impeachment of a president is surely not be a good historical memory for the Korean people, but there is no doubt that the candle light movement has contributed to the consolidation of Korean democracy. Particularly with respect to political participation, the experience has been revolutionary in the sense that ordinary citizens have come to realize that they can make a difference in politics if they have a strong motivation for political engagement. The impeachment experience simultaneously revealed both the strengths and weaknesses of the Korean political system. With respect to direct democracy, it showed the potential for high levels of participation. But in terms of representative democracy, it showed the malfunctioning of Korean political system.

According to the South Korean Constitution, there are two key steps required to impeach the existing President: a 2/3 vote of the parliament and a 2/3 vote of judges of Constitutional Court of Korea. It is a somewhat complex process that is unlikely to succeed because the collapse of the presidency inevitably brings about social instability. The Choi Soon-sil scandal began to be publicized in late October 2016. South Koreans subsequently took to the streets for several months, driving lawmakers to cast ballots to impeach Park on December 9, 2016.

The National Assembly voted to impeach Park by a vote of 234 to 56. At the beginning, nobody believed that candles could make a difference, with the pro-impeachment forces instead calling for a full-scale civil revolution. But, the anti-Park candlelight vigils continued to grow after the scandal grew to reveal the extent of the wrongdoing and Park refused to resign. The fact that Choi, as a close confidant to the President, abused presidential power through influence-peddling and embezzlement of public funds made people angry. Unbelievably, Choi did not hold any official government positions, yet was able to manipulate the function of government from behind the scenes. Over time, the rallies grew larger and larger, with Park apologizing several times and opposition politicians joining the public demonstrations.

Finally, the Constitutional Court of Korea upheld impeachment with an 8-0 unanimous vote on March 10, 2017. The court upheld the impeachment because Park admitted to having abused her authority in helping Choi garner donations from big business groups to divert millions of dollars to foundations she ran. Park, who was the first female president of South Korea, also became the first to be ousted as a result of impeachment. A new election to replace the ousted president—required by law to be held within 60 days—was held on May 9, 2017.

The causes of the crisis of representative democracy can be summarized as follows.

First, it should be pointed out that there is profound political distrust among Korean people. In almost every public survey, one of the most consistent findings is that the level of trust in politicians, the National Assembly and political parties is extremely low compared to other social institutions/entities. It seems that public distrust in governing institutions has deeper historical roots that will be difficult to overcome in the short term.

Second, from an institutional standpoint, it can be argued that political parties are not responsive to the people. Namely, they do not play enough of a role in representing the interests of ordinary citizens and generally fail to link policies and people.

Third, a feature of Korean culture could be one of the primary

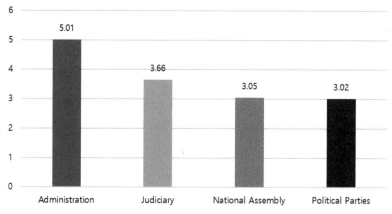

Figure 1-1. Trust in Social Institutions (mean score)

explanatory factors in the crisis of Korean democracy. Many historical case examples demonstrate that the Korean people are very participatory in the running of national and local affairs. In one sense, it could be considered a cultural asset that the Korean people consistently resist unfair and authoritarian government.

According to Cho and his associates (2019), the Korean people tend to prefer "the democratic and participatory mass culture." Their research found that the crisis of representative democracy in Korea is caused not only by the failure of party responsiveness but also by participatory cultural aspects. They also found that 70% of Koreans prefer 'democracy' to other types of government. About 20% of Korean people tend to prefer 'authoritarianism' in certain conditions. The rate for Koreans' support for democracy is 65.3%, while it is 8.7% for authoritarianism and 26.0% for 'hybrids'.

Based on two measures that capture preferences on a democracy-authoritarianism continuum and a participatory-representative continuum, it is interesting to find that Korean people prefer 'participatory democracy' (52%) to 'representative democracy' (14%). On the other hand, 9% of the people chose 'Representative Non-Democracy' and 25% 'Populist Non-Democracy'.

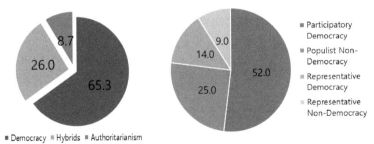

Figure 1-2. Preferred Types of Political System   Figure 1-3. Preferred Forms of Democracy

According to the authors, it is striking to find that a preference for direct democracy is dominant over the other three forms of government. The authors suggest this implies a generally contentious Korean democracy that it is "pressured by strong participatory democrats on the one hand and faces populist non-democratic aspirations on the other." They conclude that unstable democracy in Korea is partly due to democratic and participatory nature of Korean culture, especially among young and educated people.

According to a survey by Naeilshinmoon, nine out of ten Koreans support participatory democracy. They agree with having a national referendum on any controversial issue at the national level (2017.11.13.). This finding suggests that Koreans have a strong eagerness to participate directly in the policymaking process. This survey further shows that people who do not feel as if they are being represented by the existing political system are more likely to demand a participatory democracy. This suggests that if the current system of representation worked properly, the demand for the direct democracy would decrease. All of this leads to the conclusion that the key to solving the crisis of representative democracy in Korea is to make representation work.

The most recent government attempt in participatory democracy has received much attention. It began with a public debate commission regarding the Shin Kori-5 and Shin Kori-6 reactors. The key operating procedure in this process was to conduct a public opinion survey with a group of citizen jurors on conflicting national issues. Through this process, the commission reached a conclusion to stop nuclear energy in the near future, even though this has been a contentious issue with strong voices on both sides. The public debate commission operated by the government leaves open the possibility of participatory democracy in order to improve public representation.

The second attempt to strengthen public representation was to allow petitioning by ordinary citizens via the homepage of the Korean Blue House. The presidential office has promised to provide a response within 30 days to any public petition that exceeds 200,000 signatures. The public petition system, initiated on August 19, 2017, has accepted and responded to numerous petitions thus far. This petition system has also demonstrated the eagerness of the Korean people to participate in conflicting political and social affairs.

A third, social, effort to upgrade political representation has been to reform the electoral system. It is widely thought, and evidence suggests, that the Korean-style single member plurality system for selecting winners of elections is favorable to large political parties, implying a disadvantage to minor parties. This disadvantage was considered so striking that it recently led to the first reforms to the South Korean electoral system since the 1987 democratic movement. The electoral reform bill, passed by the National Assembly on Dec. 27, 2019, introduced a new electoral system that is more adaptive and representative to the interests of voters. Under the new system, voters still cast two ballots: one for 253 single member districts on a first-past-the-post basis and the other for the remaining 47 seats allocated through proportional representation (PR) through a national-level vote for a party. The party vote decides the number of seats allocated to each party out of the 300 total seats not applied to the 47 PR seats. The new system is different from the previous one in its calculation of 30 out of the 47 seats.

The old system can be defined as a 'parallel system,' while the new system is interlocking between district seats and PR seats. It is 'interlocking' because the party votes decide the total 300 seats, including the 253 district seats. It could also be considered 'semi-interlocking' because a party can obtain only 50 percent of originally allocated PR

Table 1-1. 2019 Electoral Reforms

Old system	New system (revised in Dec. 2019)
*Casting two ballots by voters • first ballot (253 single member districts on a first-past-the-post basis) • second ballot (47 proportional representation seats through a national-level vote for a party)	
Parallel system	Interlocking system (between district seats and PR seats)
• The party vote decides the number of seats allocated to each party applied only to 47 PR seats	• Identical to the old system, the party vote decides the number of seats allocated to each party applied to 17 out of the 47 PR seats.
	• 30 PR seats are allocated via an interlocking system and only 50 percent are allocated via 'semi' interlocking
• Lack of proportional representation due to a large portion of district seats • More favorable to major parties	• more representative and more favorable to minor parties

seats. Here, the total number of PR seats is 30 from the interlocking system. Although it may be somewhat limited, the new system is more representative and favorable to minor parties by distributing seats based on the number of votes obtained proportionally.

However, counter to its original purpose, the reformed electoral system can result in an unfair distribution of seats. Two major parties have established 'satellite parties' to garner more proportional representation seats. The satellite parties only field PR candidates. As a result of this gaming of the system by the major parties, the new electoral system does not properly distribute seats according to the intentions of the reforms. It seems clear that South Korean major-party politicians are not prepared to concede their vested interests to minor parties. The new 'interlocking' electoral system was introduced to ensure better representation, but resulted in a near a failure because of the unforeseen reactions by the major parties. Furthermore, in addition to the satellite parties, numerous new minor parties were created, resulting in a final

Figure 1-4. A Ballot for Proportional Representation Seats (2020 National Assembly election)

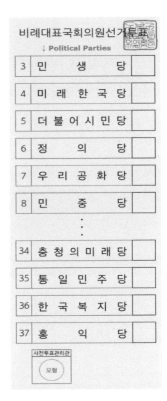

tally of 37 party names on the ballot list.

It is true that representative democracy in the world has been facing unprecedented challenges. The primary reason for the global crisis of representation has been the large gap between the representative and the ordinary citizen. According to the so-called 'principal-agent theory', the representatives—as agents—have not been appropriately playing their roles with respect to the principals—the Korean people—because they have put their own interests first. South Korea has been experiencing a representation crisis since the 1987 democratic movement. On the other hand, it is also true that the Korean people have demonstrated the participatory nature of their political culture at the same time. In conclusion, it can be argued that while Korean representative democracy may be in crisis, Korea may be experiencing a complementary chance to consolidate participatory democracy. Democracy in South Korea is still in a cycle of challenges and responses.

02

South Korea's Democracy Divided:
How Polarization Endangers Democracy?

Jeeyoung Park
Myongji University

1. Introduction

Democracy is a political system that is regulated and whose day-to-day functions are carried out by political parties. Political parties are key institutions of modern democracy. To function well as a democratic system, political parties should properly follow democratic values and norms. Further, they should always be committed to the achievement of democratic values. Parties offer citizens a choice in governance and a chance to hold the government accountable by competing in elections. When citizens join their favorite political parties, volunteer their time, donate money, and vote for their leaders, they are exercising their fundamental democratic rights. The participation of citizens in political parties offers unique benefits, including opportunities to influence policy choices, choose and engage political leaders, and run for office.

However, according to Freedom House's annual Freedom in the World report from 2018,[1] countries that suffered democratic setbacks outnumbered those that registered gains. Recent developments in democracies around the world make clear that polarization is a crucial part of this crisis. Although partisan loyalties and differing programmatic visions among voters can help stabilize a party system, polarization routinely weakens respect for democratic norms, corrodes basic legislative processes, undermines the nonpartisan stature of the judiciary, and fuels public disaffection with political parties.[1]

Recent Gallup analyses[2] show just how much our political identity is a part of our views on a wide variety of other aspects of life, many of which are not directly related to politics. Specifically, an individual's political identity affects their views of the healthcare system, how one evaluates the state of the economy, one's overall satisfaction with the way things are going in the nation, views of national security, worries about the education system, job satisfaction, outlook on the state of the environment and views of one's personal life situation. According to Iyengar et al. (2019, 129), ordinary people "increasingly dislike and distrust those from the other party." They term this phenomenon of animosity between the parties as affective polarization, and argue that its origin is the power of partisanship as a social identity. Put another way, we increasingly dislike the political "other" with both our head and our heart, and the consequences of polarization extend beyond the political domain, spilling over to our social relationships. As a result, pernicious polarization may prevent the democratic progress and promote paralysis on the important issues facing the world.

South Korean politics are also becoming more polarized. Conservative and liberal parties have almost diametrically opposed views and

---

[1] https://freedomhouse.org/report/freedom-world/freedom-world-2018

[2] https://news.gallup.com/opinion/polling-matters/215210/partisan-differences-growing-number-issues.aspx

advocate quite different policies. Growing partisan-ideological polarization within the South Korean electorate today at least partially results from the corruption scandal and impeachment of then-President Park Geun-hye in 2016-2017. In the wake of the scandal becoming public, the candlelight protesters demanded that President Park be held accountable for her actions. After her impeachment, however, pro-Park demonstrations grew, resulting in conflict between the two groups: anti-Park protesters (candlelight vigils) vs. pro-Park protesters (taegukgi rallies). Historically, South Korean civil society has long been divided by ideological orientations and age groups, and Park's impeachment once again brought these divisions to the forefront.

In this paper, I explore how polarization can produce harmful effects on democracy. First, I summarize the basic concept of democracy and polarization, and then I explain the relationship between polarization and democracy in South Korea. Finally, I suggest possible solutions to polarization for a better democracy.

2. Democracy

The origin of the word "democracy" is a composite of the Greek words demos and kratos. Since demos can be translated as "the people" and kratos as "power," the root meaning of democracy is generally considered to be "the power of the people," which is the authority to decide matters by majority rule. Some scholars have offered various definitions. For example, Schmitter and Karl (1991) define "modern political democracy" as "a system of governance in which rulers are held accountable for their actions in the public realm by citizens acting indirectly through the competition and cooperation of their elected representatives." Huntington (1991) "defines a twentieth-century political system as democratic to the extent that its most powerful collective decision-makers are selected through fair, honest, and periodic elections in which candidates freely compete for votes, and in which virtually all the adult population is eligible to vote." Although the various definitions of democracy have stimulated a large amount of scholarly debate, a true democracy must consist of "government of all the people, by all the people, and for all the people."

However, there is no guarantee that a majority of the people will make fair decisions all of the time. For instance, certain decisions may be unfair to minorities; indeed, a ruling majority could systematically ignore minority interests. Achen and Bartels (2016) argue in their book Democracy for Realists that voters tend to base their decision-making on partisan loyalties, leaving the current democratic system open to exploitation by powerful, unscrupulous actors.

3. Polarization

Polarization implies the existence of two conflicting forces or groups that are usually opposites; that is, groups that hold values, principles, interests, and ideologies that are perceived as incompatible and exclusionary. The differences between the groups tend to stimulate conflict and make it difficult to achieve the ideological, political, and social consensus needed for democratic governance. In the extreme form of polarization, where principles, interests, or ideologies are perceived as antagonistic, attempts to eliminate or suppress the "other"—frequently considered an enemy—may justify exclusion and the use of violence (Mallen and García-Guadilla 2017; McCoy et al. 2018).

Some scholars argue that political polarization is associated with both democratic strengthening and democratic erosion (Somer and McCoy 2018). Polarization can help to strengthen political parties and institutionalize party systems because it enables them to mobilize voters around identifiable differences. Offering voters clear choices and serving as heuristic cues about policy positions can be helpful for citizen decision making. Polarization is also potentially transformative in its capacity to address an imbalance in the popular vs. oligarchic versions of democracy (Slater 2013; Stavrakakis 2018). Thus, polarization can serve democratization when used by political actors equipped with an inclusive agenda to contain it before it turns pernicious. However, polarizing politics always carries the risk of taking on a life of its own, eviscerating cross-cutting ties and nonpartisan channels for compromise, and becoming detrimental. Polarizing challengers often provoke an elite backlash and counter-mobilization to stymie their transformative attempts, rather than a recognition of their reformist and inclusionary potential in building a constructively agonistic and pluralist democracy (Stavrakakis 2018). This elite backlash, in turn, can motivate the polarizing challengers to double down and strive to protect themselves by changing the rules and creating hegemonic power. Thus, whether polarization serves a constructive or destructive purpose for democracy depends on the behaviors of both incumbents and opponents, new political actors and traditionally dominant groups.

In particular, political identity can become all-encompassing as people view those in the "other" group with distrust, suspicion, or fear, and cease to interact with them, even segregating themselves in their neighborhoods, social relationships, and newsfeeds with like-minded people. The dividing line between the groups may be simply support of, or opposition to, a personalistic political leader. Furthermore, group identity is the key, linking citizens to a particular leader or partisan identity. Ideological strife is a perennial source of material for election campaigns and partisan bickering in South Korea.

4. Polarization and Democracy in South Korea

Since South Korea transitioned to democracy with political liberalization and direct presidential elections in 1987, all realms of South Korean society have democratized. Recently, the impeachment process of Park demonstrated the combined forces of democracy of the public square and representative democracy. In the Fall of 2016, representatives drew on the public's anger expressed on the streets and in the public square and voted to impeach Park. The Constitutional Court subsequently convicted President Park, expelling her from office. In the presidential election campaign that followed, the candidates competed with policies aimed at dealing with the demands and dissatisfaction of the public. As a result, Moon Jae-in was elected president on May 9, 2017. That is, elected representatives accepted the demands of the square, and this enabled democratic processes to continue peacefully. Citizens whose candles lit up the public square put pressure on representatives and representative democracy by bringing about the election of a new president.

However, as the scandal headed towards the impeachment ruling, conservatives and pro-Park supporters rallied against the candlelight protests supporting Park's case. The counter-protests by Park supporters argued that Park was not guilty because she did not personally take any bribes. While the anti-Park rallies have drawn people of all ages, the pro-Park rallies are less diverse. Their supporters are mainly the older generation, and many of them proudly place themselves at the conservative pole of South Korea's long-polarized political spectrum. They are ardently anti-communist and pro-U.S., and they believe that what they are doing is for the protection of liberal democracy.

The different behaviors and beliefs of the two groups represent the deep political divide in South Korea over the meanings of patriotism,

Korean identity, and democracy. Each side views the opposing political party and its supporters as a threat to the nation or their way of life if that other party gains power. For that reason, the incumbent party's followers have grown to tolerate more illiberal and increasingly authoritarian behavior to stay in power, while the opponents have become increasingly willing to resort to undemocratic means to remove them from power.

What makes a society become more polarized? The root causes can be found in the polarization of people's perceptions. In an age of material abundance and popularization of information technology, people can access limitless information. People are increasingly able to interpret information in their own ways, and form their views based on those interpretations, without encountering the traditional elite filtering mechanisms. In this new information environment, controversial "news" with little to no factual support has proliferated (Allcot and Gentzkow 2017; Bradshaw and Howard 2017; Lazer et al. 2018). Such information has spread widely via social media, where individuals can easily create and distribute stories. Under these circumstances, content creators and consumers have confidence in their own perception and views. Social media enables people to share the news with like-minded people, potentially creating an echo-chamber effect (Sunstein 2001; Bakshy et al. 2015). Moreover, individuals with extreme political views can use social media not only to consume but also to distribute selective news.

5. Conclusion

The most effective and lasting solution to political polarization is that people should recognize the fact that individuals' views on political issues are determined by his or her perceptions and beliefs, and not necessarily on any absolute truth. The truth is that in politics, there is no absolute truth. Democracy, in a sense, is the process of compromise.

Looking back on our history, South Korea's democracy is among the most resilient in the world. When political institutions failed to prevent the corruption of an insulated elite, ordinary citizens intervened. While populism runs roughshod over democratic institutions elsewhere, South Korea's democracy has demonstrated a capacity to overcome serious challenges. South Korea's democracy stands out as remarkable, even though there are strong elements of continuity from the past that impose restrictions on which voices gain representation. Based on historical experience, we can learn the importance of caring for our democracy.

This is a critical juncture in South Korea's democratic consolidation, where a sustainable direct democracy that complements the existing representative democracy could be created as a route toward a truly mature democracy. This road toward resetting the nation will not be easy. Nevertheless, South Korea has acquired many valuable lessons from the scandal that led to the first-ever impeachment of our president. Now it is the time for South Koreans to reflect on how to use the power of the people to build the advanced democracy they wish to realize in the future.

03

Democracy in Crisis?
Evidence from South Korea

Dong-Joon Jung

Inha University

1. Introduction

In recent years, one of the most widely discussed topics in the political science literature has been the crisis of democracy (Jung 2020a;
Kurlantzick 2014; Levitsky and Ziblatt 2018; Mounk 2018; Przeworski
2019). It has not been rare to see democratic regimes break down when
they are at their rudimentary stages, as we have witnessed with many
young democracies in Latin America during the second half of the 20th
century, in the post-communist Soviet region in the early 2000s, and
in the Middle East over the past decade. These governments were initiated with a number of democratic deficits that set them up to be short-
lived. What makes today's discussion of the crisis of democracy new,
however, is that we now see such democratic deficits—which had been
considered the legacies of former authoritarian regimes—among many
mature democracies in Europe and in the United States as well. Even
those young democracies that were once regarded as 'consolidated' in

Eastern Europe and East Asia, have shown signs of democratic derailing, although the degree of the derailment varies from country to country. What we see today with regard to the crisis of democracy, therefore, is a global phenomenon.

Many scholars have sought to discover the origins of this new crisis and how to fix it. As this chapter will discuss, party elites and their polarization have been identified as one of the culprits. As their socioeconomic backgrounds and ideological positions have come to more closely align with their partisan identities, and as political parties developed more extreme and partisan-based policy programs, the voice of the political center that accounts for the majority of constituents has seen its influence decrease, contributing to the problem of democratic representation. The failure of parties, especially mainstream parties, to respond to a wide swath of society gives birth to the conditions under which populist movements can grow. Across Europe over the past decade, there has been a surge of populist movements (whether right or left), and many of those have turned into party organizations, some of which have achieved substantial electoral successes. This lack of representation combined with the rise of populism inevitably divides society, creating "social polarization" (Mason 2018), where people with similar social identities gather together and fall into an antagonistic relationship with groups having different backgrounds.

This chain of events associated with the crisis of democracy are also present in today's South Korean politics. South Korea has been regarded as one of the most successfully democratized countries, as three decades have passed since its break from its former status as a military dictatorship. Unlike other countries in South Korea's democratization cohort—such as, for instance, Poland and Hungary, whose democracy is being challenged under the leadership of populist right-wing parties—South Korea seems to have navigated well amid the storm of democratic crisis currently striking the globe. The 2016-2017 candlelight protests and subsequent impeachment of former president Park Geun-hye have attracted worldwide attention and been acclaimed as an exemplar of the victory of grassroots democracy over a corrupt leader.

Ironically, however, this victory served as a trigger that has deepened the existing social cleavages of Korean society, particularly partisan cleavages. It is party elites who are on the front line politically to take advantage of such divisions. In particular, the former Liberty Korea party (now transformed as the United Future party) that president Park belonged to, has painted themselves as politically victimized and responded with a great deal of antagonism. The party leaders have continued to publicly make populist and hateful remarks and have tried to rally their supporters around the flag. This populist movement from the major conservative party in South Korea, though it might have succeeded to increase popularity among its own supporters, has grown to be at odds with the overall preferences of the ideological center-right, who are starting to feel that their political interests are largely left unrepresented. It has also contributed to arousing ordinary citizens' feelings of antagonism toward the opposite partisan groups, thus further increasing social polarization (Jang and Suh 2019; Jung 2018). As this partisan and social polarization deepens, some have begun raising concerns about the crisis of South Korean democracy (Park and Yoon 2019).

Numerous studies have dealt with ways to overcome the ongoing crises. Some have taken an institutional approach to try to fix the malfunctioning of representative institutions. For instance, more direct and open measures of political participation, like referendums, have been sought so as to complement the weak representation of political mediation (Altman 2017). Since such direct democratic mechanisms can sometimes become the weapon of populist movements (Mudde 2016b), however, other institutional methods such as judicial review by constitutional courts have been relied upon as the final bulwark of democracy (Staton et al. 2018). On the other hand, other scholars have asserted that the institutional approach cannot be a sufficient measure for protecting democracy and have instead called for "unwritten democratic norms" (Ziblatt and Levitsky 2018) to take root in both the elites and citizens to ensure that democracy becomes the only game in town (Bugarič 2019; Mason 2018).

This chapter reviews the previous literature that has examined the questions of where the crisis of democracy has come from and how to overcome it, and seeks to apply the discussions to the South Korean case to evaluate whether and to what extent South Korean democracy is in danger. Through this, we can see the current status of South Korean democracy in perspective and develop proper prescriptions for its shortcomings.

2. Where Has the Crisis of Democracy Come from?

Party polarization

Today's crisis of democracy can first and foremost be attributed to partisan polarization at the elite level. We have seen an increase in partisan divides at parliaments in many democracies over the past decades (Jung 2018). A number of studies on the American Congress have come to the general conclusion that inter-party distance has widened between the Democratic and Republican parties, whereas intra-party cohesion has tightened (Bafumi and Shapiro 2009; Davis et al. 2014; Levendusky 2009; McGhee et al. 2014; Jones 2010; Iyengar et al. 2012). These studies almost unanimously argue that "few dispute that Congress is polarized at historic levels and continues to grow more so each year" (McGhee et al. 2014). As congressmen become more partisan, their ideological positions on policy issues become more divergent; with the Democrats more likely vote for liberal bills and the Republicans more likely do the opposite, making their ideological and policy positions more clearly aligned with their partisanship (Jones 2010). Such party polarization has accelerated since the U.S. Presidency has been held by Donald Trump, who has continued publicly to make provocative remarks through social media and seek far-right policies on many social issues.

Europe has been no exception with respect to this elite polarization, as party positions move either to the right or to the left. As post-materialistic values on an array of social issues—such as regional integration, abortion, homosexuality, and the environment—have shaped West European politics over the past generations from the left, conservative parties, largely in response, have made a right turn, emphasizing the negative consequences of those progressive values: how EU integration and mass immigration jeopardize their economic and physical security, and how multinationalism and homosexuality disrupt their family and traditions (Cole 2005). Eastern Europe has also seen a rise of right-wing politics, particularly among mainstream parties such as Fidesz in Hungary and Law and Justice in Poland, although their right turn should be understood less as a reaction to the diffusion of post-materialistic values than as a regression toward traditional values that remained largely latent, but have once again come to the forefront as a result of the economic crises that hit the region during the late 2000s (Bugarič 2019; Koev 2015; Mudde 2016a).

In particular, political polarization among mainstream parties is problematic for representative democracy in that the ideological center that consists of the majority of the constituents can be underrepresented by such polarized party positions (Jung 2020a). While leaving the voice of the majority unheard, party polarization at best rallies the more partisan supporters by responding only to their interests, and in many cases ends up giving birth to a bitterly divided society in which groups with different social identities hate each other, as will be discussed below. As those in the political center get frustrated, they are likely to lose their faith in the mainstream political system and become indifferent to politics in general. At worst, they could start questioning how their democracy works and look for alternatives, eventually leading to the breakdown of democratic systems (Linz 1978; Linz and Stepan 1996).

How does South Korea fit into this discussion then? Recent studies on the National Assembly of South Korea reveal that there has been an increase in partisan polarization at the parliamentary level. Ka (2014; 2016), in his work on the 16th to 19th National Assemblies, claims that the ideological positions of the legislators has become more and more polarized during the period culminating in the 19th National Assembly. He attributes this polarization largely to strong party leadership with a primary authority on candidate nomination forcing its members to have a clear ideological stance. Kang (2012) also contends that the ideological distance between parties in the 19th National Assembly has widened compared to previous assemblies, and that policy areas where such polarization occurs extends from traditional issues like security to economic and post-material issues. Jung (2017) also finds, based on survey data of National Assembly members, evidence of partisan polarization emerging at the level of the parliament. In effect, South Korean politics has been deeply divided along partisan lines ever since former president Park's impeachment. Political deadlocks over many issues, including electoral reforms that introduce more elements of proportional representation and the creation of the Senior Civil Servant Corruption Investigation Unit that checks against the power of the prosecution, have hindered the National Assembly from performing its legislative role.

Such deepened polarization among party elites can lay the groundwork for the crisis of democracy by making citizens distrust their representatives (Lee, J.M. 2019). As reported in Table 3-1, the Public Attitudes about Political Parties and Social Integration survey by SSK-Myungji University shows that citizens give more positive ratings to their democracy and government in 2018 compared to 2015 when President Park was in office. The results imply that the more they experience the power of the people to change their politics, the more confidence they give to their own democratic systems. To the contrary, however, their trust in the legislature and the parties has decreased greatly. Given the finding of a recent study that elite polarization is associated with increasing distrust in the legislature among South Koreans (Seo 2016), such a decrease in trust could have been caused, at least in part, by party polarization in the legislature.

Table 3-1. The mean comparisons of South Koreans' attitudes toward their democracy and representative institutions

Year surveyed	Satisfaction with democracy (1: Very unsatisfactory to 4: Very satisfactory)	Trust in government (0: Do not trust at all to 10: Trust completely)	Trust in legislature (0: Do not trust at all to 10: Trust completely)	Trust in party (0: Do not trust at all to 10: Trust completely)
2015	2.39	4.82	3.66	3.66
2018	2.48	5.01	3.05	3.02

Note: The survey was conducted in 2017 as well but the question was not asked.

The rise of populism

One of the consequences of the failure of mainstream parties to respond to a wider society is the rise of populism, which has been particularly prevalent in Europe over the past couple of decades (Jung 2020a; 2020b; Mudde 2016). Cas Mudde (2016), in his book on extremism and populist parties in Europe, defines populism as "a thin-centered ideology that considers society to be ultimately separated into two homogeneous and antagonistic groups, 'the people' and 'the corrupt elite', and … argues that politics should be an expression of the volonté general (general will) of the people" (68). Populists regard a society as consisting of "the people" that are homogenous in nature. They take it as a moral issue to make their voices heard to the fullest, rejecting the idea that there is a more sophisticated and privileged group who should guide the actions of a larger group that is largely ignorant of politics and policy and tends to make more emotional decisions. They are thus, in essence, anti-pluralist and anti-elitist.

Furthermore, populist parties are not distinguishable by their ideological positions; indeed, there are versions of populism on both the left and the right (Mudde 2016, 68). Europe in particular has seen a surge of populist movements in recent years. Some of these movements have transitioned into political parties and achieved some degree of success in many national and European elections. These include the Pirate Parties in Northern and Central Europe, Podemos in Spain, and Five Star Movement in Italy from the left[1] and Lega Nord in Italy, National Rally in France, Freedom Party of Austria, and Jobbik in Hungary from the right (Jung 2020a). Of course, most of these are niche parties looking for political support from those not well represented by mainstream

---

[1] The Five Star Movement is considered to have some right-wing policy stances.

parties, and their electoral margins do not seem to be threatening those mainstream parties yet.[2] However, given that most European countries are parliamentary systems combined with some form of proportional representation (i.e., where small parties also have political leverage), the rise of populist parties could change European politics in a direction that jeopardizes the existence of liberal democracy.

South Korea may not be a safety zone for the rise of populism either. In a nutshell, the 20th South Korean National Assembly is primarily composed of mainstream moderate parties, most representatively, the incumbent Democratic Party and its main opponent, the United Future Party, whose seats combined account for 81.7% of the total seats (245 out of 300) as of March 2020. Of the parties listed on the ballot, perhaps the Justice Party and Liberty Republican Party could be regarded as extreme parties (left and right, respectively), but they have won only eight combined seats (6 and 2, respectively). On its surface, thus, there may be no serious worries yet about the rise of populist parties in South Korean politics. Given that populist parties are not necessarily limited to small niche parties, however, our focus should be less on what the parties are called in a party family than on how they actually behave. As Mudde (2016) emphasizes, the populist turn of mainstream parties can be far more dangerous than populist niche parties, as the former holds legal rights and potentially the power to realize what they want to implement (13-15).

From this consideration, a series of populist remarks recently made by the leadership of mainstream parties in South Korea could turn their politics populist. For instance, the leaders of the formerly-named

---

[2] Five Star Movement who entered government after the 2018 Italian general election may be an exception.

Liberty Korea party such as Hong Jun-pyo and Na Kyung-won, since losing their incumbent status after the impeachment of President Park, have continued to use a strategy of victimizing themselves and rallying their supporters by means of populist rhetoric. One of the populist strategies often used is to refer to their supporters "the people" and claim legitimacy by insisting that they are just following the popular will. However, does the popular will actually exist? Given that the term "the people" consists of different individuals' varied preferences, it may not be feasible to define the popular will in a simple way (Prendergast 2019). Dividing society into the people and the rest and only referring to one's in-group members as the people is thus populist (Jung 2020b). As these leaders continue to seek populist strategies as such, divisive and antagonistic discourse can be constructed and disseminated to consolidate the political grounds of populist parties.

In turn, the limited available data shows that this type of elite-made populist rhetoric is also driving ordinary citizens to form populist attitudes. For example, the battery of questions from the 2018 Unification Perception Survey regarding attitudes toward foreign immigrants, which is known to gauge the nativist attitudes of citizens (Mudde 2016, 8-9), reveals that there has been a turn to nativist attitudes in recent years; more disagree with the statement that "having a coexistence of diverse races, religions, and cultures is good to have in every country" and more agree with the statement that "the acceptance of different nationalities as citizens harms a country's cohesion." (Jung et al. 2018, 171-172). Demand for government authority, another attitudinal dimension of populism, is also found to have increased, according to the SSK-Myungji University data. To the question of, "assemblies and demonstrations can be restricted for the sake of government authority and the success of policies," on a scale from 1 (strongly disagree) to 4 (strongly agree), the mean response changes from 2.18 in 2017 to 2.36 in 2018. In sum, it can be said that, in recent years, South Korean politics is being influenced by populism at both the elite and citizen levels.

Social polarization

Party elite polarization and the subsequent rise of populism inevitably leads to social division among citizens. Although scholars disagree on whether citizens are ideologically polarized, thus reducing the size of the ideological center in number (Kevins and Soroka 2018; Iyengar et al. 2012; Jung 2018), a consensus seems to have developed that they are affectively divided along their social identities, including socioeconomic classes, regions, religions, ethnicities, and so on (Iyengar et al. 2019; Jang and Seo 2019; Mason 2015; 2018). And as those social cleavages become aligned with their partisan allegiances, they become sorted into "very different kinds of people" (Mason 2018, 31). Mason (2015; 2018) terms such social division as 'social polarization,' distinguishing it from 'issue polarization,' in which citizens increasingly disagree on policy issues along partisanship lines. Such social sorting also induces affective polarization, meaning that people's affect becomes more hostile to opposing groups. In such a socially-polarized society, it should be difficult to achieve a consensus on any important policy issues through democratic means of decision-making, which could in turn lead to a crisis of democracy.

Social polarization can take various forms, one of which is the notion of 'negative partisanship' defined as "negative feelings toward the opposing party" (Abramowitz and Webster 2016, 14). In effect, empirical evidence reveals that the size of partisans at the aggregate level has dwindled since the mid-20th century, as the role of parties as a political mediator has weakened in consequence of a series of socioeconomic changes like economic development, the growth of the middle class and increased levels of education (Bell 2000; Dalton 2007; Franklin et al. 1992). Such weakening partisanship appears to be contradictory to what we are witnessing today in the sense of social polarization, but Abramowitz and Webster (2016) explain this contradiction as negative partisanship simply substituting for the decrease in importance of its positive counterpart. A recent study on South Korea also finds that there is a great deal of negative partisanship among citizens. Jung (2018) reveals that those reporting negative partisanship outnumber their positive counterparts in the survey analyzed and that the electoral effect of negative partisanship is greater than that of positive partisanship (164-165).

However, as emotions can be "sorted into very basic positive and negative dimensions" (Huddy et al. 2015, 3), and positive feelings toward one does not necessarily lead to negative feelings toward the opposite (Cacioppo et al. 1997), feelings toward various political parties also can be positive and/or negative, or neither. In this sense, social polarization can be described as an increase in positive partisanship toward the parties with whom people identify and/or in negative partisanship toward the opposing parties. Mason (2018) creates such an indicator intended to gauge the level of partisan prejudice in the American electorates, termed as 'warmth bias,' which is the "levels of the difference between the two party-feeling thermometers" (51), and finds that warmth bias among Americans has increased over time over the past 30 years (47-59).

To create a similar indicator in South Korean terms, I employ the SSK-Myungji University survey items about respondents' feelings toward the two major parties, the Democratic Party and formerly Liberty Korea Party, measured on an eleven-point scale from 0 (dislike very

Table 3-2. Difference between two-party feelings ('warmth bias')

Year surveyed	2015	2017	2018
For all respondents	2.37	4.17	4.85
Only for partisans	3.61	6.59	6.99

Note: The index ranges from 0 to 10.

much) to 10 (like very much). Warmth bias, following Mason's lead, is calculated as the absolute difference between each respondent's feeling rating of the two parties (51). The results shown in Table 3-2 suggest that a similar trend is found in South Korea as well; feelings toward the two parties has become more polarized over the past years. Restricting the sample to participants who responded that they do indeed identify with a party the gap has even more sharply widened. These results may be in part because a moderate faction of formerly Liberty Korea Party split off and formed a new party, the Bareun Party, in January 2017, just before the 2017 survey was conducted. Nevertheless, it seems clear that people's feelings toward their own and opposing parties have become more biased and polarized in recent years.

3. How to Make It Work?

Direct democracy mechanisms

Today's crisis of democracy can be equated with the crisis of political mediation (Gerbaudo 2019b). As Pitkin, the classical thinker on democratic representation, admits, representative democracy inevitably bears incongruence between the representatives and citizens since it is impractical for all members of a society to participate in the political decision-making process in today's mass politics (Pitkin 1967). However, as mainstream parties fail to be sensitive to the majority of the electorate, and as populist parties politically take advantage of such situations by arguing they act in the name of "the people," the distance between the representatives and citizens should widen enough to bring the crisis to the system itself. Mounk (2018) in his discussion on "rights without democracy" criticizes 'elitism' by contending that democracy betrays itself when the rights to make decisions on major national policies become concentrated in the hands of a small number of party elites, technocrats, and businessmen (53-98). Again, therefore, today's crisis of democracy in essence comes from the failure of representation, that is, political mediation.

If political mediation is the core of the problem, the way to get around it may be simple: avoid mediation and adopt more direct and open participation using direct democratic mechanisms such as referendums and popular initiatives (Jung 2020a). Altman (2017) defines direct democratic mechanisms as "a publicly recognized institution wherein citizens decide or express their opinions on issues—other than through legislative and executive elections—directly at the ballot box through universal and secret vote" (1209). Such institutional mechanisms are, at least in theory, expected to complement the shortfalls of representative democracy, as they can bring more people into the decision-making processes and make more diverse voices heard (Kaufmann et al. 2010). If parties increasingly fail to represent their constituents, direct democracy mechanisms can be an alternative means of increasing the quality of democratic representation (Qvortrup 2014). In practice, the use of referendums has indeed been on the increase over the past 30 years across the world (Altman 2017; Prato and Strulovici 2017; Tierney 2012).

As another way of resolving the problem of political mediation, more recently, parties have sought to take advantage of the development of technology by actively adopting social media platforms into their decision-making processes. They use social media platforms as part of strategies ranging from distribution of original digital media production for campaign mobilization (Booth et al. 2018; Findlay et al. 2019; Nyabola 2018) to opening their intra-party decision making to rank-and-file party members (Gerbaudo 2019a; 2019b; Lee, J.M. 2019; Park and Yoon 2019; Schradie 2019). Regarding the former, it has already become popular for parties, whether mainstream or niche, to use digital content created by their 'fans' to generate everyday political discourse during their campaigns. The use of digital media does not stop here; it is furthered by the rise of the 'digital party,' defined as a party that "professes to be more open to ordinary people, more immediate and more direct, more authentic and more transparent," and largely cultivates this image using digital platforms (Gerbaudo 2019a, 4). Examples of digital parties include the aforementioned Podemos and Five Star Movement.

South Korea has not been as notable in the space of direct democracy and self-governance. With regard to referendums, none have been held since the 1987 constitutional referendum, which produced a new presidential system with direct popular vote for a single five-year term. In addition, as an effort to enhance local autonomy and self-government, direct local elections resumed in 1991 after democratization, and a series of measures were introduced to endow local residents with the rights to call for a financial audit, develop and vote on popular initiatives and referendums, and recall governors and legislators at the local levels. In spite of such efforts, however, as Kang (2018) points out, the authorities of local governments are still restrained in many aspects (320-330). Sometimes their administrative roles are not clearly demarcated, with many subject to the veto power of the central government.

Furthermore, their funding is dependent on subsidies from the central government, and the nomination system in local elections is heavily influenced by the leadership of the parties in central government, subordinating local politics to national politics. All in all, mechanisms of direct democracy and local autonomy in South Korea cannot be considered strong.

On the positive side for South Korea, such direct democracy mechanisms are not without drawbacks. A referendum, in particular, only asks for a 'yes or no' binary response to a simple single-item statement ready-made by political elites at a time that is strategically and cautiously chosen by them, making it susceptible to manipulation in favor of those in power (Daly 2015). Measuring popular preferences in such a dichotomous way has also been criticized for its failure to capture the complex layers of varying interests, and for the zero-sum-like situation in which it would ultimately result (Walker 2003). Its responsive nature can also be criticized for its lack of deliberation; in particular, it would be practically impossible to ensure that all participants are provided the relevant information and involved in repetitive and institutionalized interactions to the degree that they take place in parliaments (Bochsler and Hug 2015).

A group of recent studies on political activism in the digital age also question whether social media and digital parties have actually empowered ordinary citizens as key decision-makers. Booth et al. (2018) discuss how the narratives of the 2016 US presidential election were infiltrated with trolling, conspiracy theories, and fake news and other falsehoods (131-158). Schradies (2019) adds to this concern by arguing that those with money and more institutionalized and professional organizations are at an advantage for maximizing the political effects of digital activism, making the gap between the power and the powerless greater rather than smaller. Gerbaudo (2019a; 2019b) also casts doubt on the democratic nature of the use of digital practices, contending that digital parties' intra-party democracy "is plebiscitarian and centralised, with a low degree of institutionalisation of rules and procedures and of inclusiveness" (2019, 2), thus failing to make their constituents more included and empowered.

Substantive democracy mechanisms

Most of all, though, direct democracy raises serious concerns about a possibility that is always a looming potential consequence of the mechanism: namely, that decisions made by the majority could be so illiberal that they erode certain core values of democracy such as political equality, civic liberty, and mutual tolerance. Further, leaving final decisions in the hands of the majority, if the majority does not want democracy, could even cause the full breakdown of a democratic regime (Kelsen 2006). This is a situation known as 'the paradox of democracy,' meaning that "a democratic regime might effectively overthrow itself, if the demos as a whole, or a sufficiently large part of it, were to turn against the democratic principle itself" (Accetti and Zuckerman 2017, 183).[3]

This paradox is closely related to which vision of democracy one wishes to emphasize—procedural democracy or substantive democracy (Belavusau 2014; Jung 2020a; Schmitt 2008). The former vision sees democracy as just another form of government with particular rules about how governments are formed and political decisions are made, giving weight to its procedural minimum (i.e., features such as majority

---

[3] Of course, this should not be a problem only for direct democracy. Even for indirect/representative democracy, if illiberal decisions are made by a small number of representatives and they are endorsed by the people, the same problem can ensue.

rule). The latter vision, on the other hand, contends that certain values make democracy democratic, and it is the primary goal of democracy to protect those values. With regard to direct democracy, the believers in procedural democracy will argue that any decisions made via proper democratic rules—such as a majority rule—should be respected regardless of how illiberal they may be. To them, direct democracy may be the most democratic mechanism, as it ensures, at least in theory, that the majority will be reflected in decision making.

To the contrary, whomever believes in the vision of substantive democracy would contend that decisions against the core values of democracy can eventually be overturned, even if they are made by the majority will. From the perspective of substantive democracy, therefore, mechanisms that draw on open and direct participation should be restrained by safety valve mechanisms that veto illiberal decisions, such as judicial review. Judicial review, as the protector of minority rights, can work as a representation-reinforcing institution (Ely 1980) in the sense that democratic representation should mean that no one's rights should be infringed upon by the others (Lever 2009). Strong judicial review in particular can annul any bills or executive orders considered unconstitutional. Judicial review in this regard can serve as "speed bumps" that slow down, if not stop, the backsliding of democracy via illiberal decisions made by democratic rule (Bugarič 2019, 614).

In South Korea, the decision made by the Constitutional Court in 2017 to impeach former President Park may be the most recent and proper example that shows how the judicial branch can work as the gatekeeper of democracy. After the National Assembly's decision to impeach the president in December 2016 for allegations of abuse of power and corruption, the Constitutional Court upheld the decision unanimously in March of 2017, officially ending the term of her presidency. From the standpoint of procedural democracy, it is legitimate for the president to have supreme decision-making authority, as he or she is directly elected by, and is thus believed to represent, the whole nation. However, when such a representative system goes off the rails (as in Park's case in which numerous governmental decisions were found to have been made by her friend, Choi Soon-sil, who had no legitimate right to do so), the constitutional court can step in and stop certain actions so as to protect the substantive values of democracy.

However, substantive institutions like judicial review also have their own limitations (Jung 2020a). First, the act of strong judicial review has been criticized from the point of view of procedural democracy, primarily because it lacks democratic legitimacy, as judges are not popularly elected representatives like governors and legislators (Waldron 1998; 2006). A counter-majoritarian decision by judicial review is against the principle of political equality captured in terms like 'one-man-one-vote,' as it gives more weight to judges who are not popularly elected, and thus not held directly accountable for their decisions (Bellamy 2007; Lever 2009). Furthermore, it is not guaranteed that judges will actually be more qualified in protecting democratic values than the other representative bodies; they are, after all, humans who are bound by certain beliefs and interests (Lenta 2004; Zurn 2002). While the aforementioned case of Park's impeachment is a positive example of judicial intervention to defend a democratic constitution, the banning of the Unified Progressive Party by the Constitutional Court in 2014 is perhaps a more controversial example that may cast a doubt on how widely the authority of the constitutional court should be delimitated (Jung 2020a).4

---

4 For more details on the debate surrounding the ban of the Unified Progressive Party,

Democratic norms as the only game in town

As such, any institutional approach—whether via direct or substantive democratic mechanisms—comes with its own limitations. Ziblatt and Levitsky (2018) contend that constitutional and democratic institutions alone neither work perfectly nor can effectively prevent democracy from derailing. Bugarič (2019) also points out the limitations of constitutional institutions arguing that they are vulnerable to populist attacks, easily becoming the political targets of illiberal leaders. All in all, there seems to be a scholarly agreement that, both in theory and in practice, democratic institutions alone cannot guarantee the perpetuation of a largely democratic system.

What should be done then? Whatever institutions a country may have, the important point is how they are run. In other words, the question is how political actors—both elites and citizens—hold on to democratic norms and values and behave accordingly. At the party elite level, Ziblatt and Levitsky (2018), in their insightful work that diagnoses the causes of the current crisis of democracy in the U.S., emphasize the role of party elites as gatekeepers of democracy that screen out potential dictators. For parties to take on the role, they should be committed to "unwritten democratic norms" that make democratic institutions work properly. These norms are, using their words, as "shared codes of conduct that become common knowledge within a particular community or society - accepted, respected, and enforced by its members (Ziblatt and Levitsky 2018, 101). Out of many kinds of norms, they specifically point out two "as fundamental to a functioning democracy: mutual tolerance and forbearance" (102); the former refers to taking the opponent groups as competitors rather than as enemies, trying to coex-

---

see Lee (2015).

ist with rather than remove them, while the latter implies restraining themselves from exercising their legal rights and political power, even when they are allowed to do so, as they acknowledge that blood will beget more blood, leading to the breakdown of the system itself.

While Ziblatt and Levitsky claim that party leaders transferring substantial power to regular voters through the democratization of candidate selection may have led to the crisis, for South Korea, this is likely not the case. On the contrary, South Korea has been criticized for endowing party leaders with too much power in intra-party decision-making processes. Ever since the Democratic Party adopted the mechanism of public participation nomination in the 2002 presidential election, a series of measures to expand public participation in the nomination system have been sought (Lee, J-J. 2019). Despite the trials and errors of the past 18 years, however, the South Korean nomination system is still heavily dependent on a handful of party leaders (Kang 2018). In some sense, in South Korea the problem is party leadership exercising power too strongly, rather than ceding power, in their intra-party decision making processes. This feature of South Korean politics can make party leadership less of a gatekeeper of democratic norms and more of a source of political/social polarization and populism, if they have incentives to do so, as previously discussed.

At the citizen level, a more active version of participatory politics is needed to overcome the crisis of representative democracy. But to simply let citizens respond to ready-made bills and policy options in a plebiscitary fashion, as discussed earlier, is not likely to be the right way forward. Instead, citizens need to be allowed to take part in every step of decision-making processes and be empowered to affect actual outcomes (Gerbaudo 2019b). However, we have also seen that such political efforts to embrace and empower their partisan supporters could easily turn into populist politics, only to lead to political and social po-larization. Therefore, the mutual tolerance and forbearance mentioned by Ziblatt and Levitsky should not only be the virtues of party elites. Healthy democratic functioning requires them to be entrenched at the bottom as well. Mason (2018) also suggests having a "new social norm" that is an open and tolerant mindset toward opposing political groups, which, in turn, allows for civilized partisan interactions (132-133). What we need is thus citizens who are active in political life, equipped with open and tolerant views.

Many empirical studies show that South Koreans are relatively actively engaged in political matters and tend to give voice to their opinions when needed. As they went through former President Park' scandal and impeachment, in particular, the level of political participa-tion dramatically increased. For instance, voter turnout was 77.2% in the 2017 presidential election, the highest in 20 years of presidential elections, and 60.2% in the 2018 local elections, the highest in 23 years of local elections. Also, there has been an increase in party membership measured as the ratio of total party members to total population (Lee, J.M. 2019, 12-14), putting aside how active those members actually are. Furthermore, more citizens are taking advantage of recent develop-ments in digital media as an outlet to express their political opinions, for instance by signing petitions for the Public Petition to the Blue House and creating and sharing political content through various social media platforms. Moreover, for today's South Korean citizens, it seems to have become a habit to take to the streets and make their voices through peaceful demonstrations.

All of these developments lead to the conclusion that the levels of political participation among present-day South Koreans cannot be said to be low. But, has such active engagement contributed to forming more open and tolerant views of fellow citizens with opposing viewpoints? That is, is tolerant and respectful citizenship internalized in the minds of today's South Koreans? The honest answer is that it is too early to conclude, but reasonable speculation is that we may be far from saying that South Koreans have become more tolerant and accepting than before, especially given the increasing populist attitudes and social polarization discussed in previous sections. Fortunately, however, as proven by the Candlelight Protests and other democratization movements through their history, South Koreans seem to hold firm beliefs in democracy as a political system. The 2017 Unification Perception Survey shows that the mean score for the item asking how much one agrees with the statement that "although democracy is not perfect, it is still better than all other political system," measured on a four-point scale (from 1: strongly disagree to 4: strongly agree), is 3.05, suggesting that most citizens acknowledge democracy as the best political system. In short, it can be said that growing social polarization and antagonism notwithstanding, South Koreans are not discarding their support for democracy.

4. Conclusion

This chapter delves into the sources of the crisis of representative democracy and discusses possible solutions, focusing on the South Korea case. The current crisis of democracy can be equated with the crisis of democratic representation, which has arisen from party polarization, populism, and subsequent social polarization. In South Korea, over the past few years, all of these symptoms have been detected, at least to some degree; there is evidence that party elites have become polarized both ideologically and affectively, bringing the legislative processes to a deadlock; that populist remarks and discourse have been made and circulated by mainstream parties, inducing ordinary citizens to form populist attitudes; and that people have subsequently become more socially divided along partisan lines. To sum up, many of the symptoms of the crisis of democracy are also being found in today's South Korean politics.

This chapter addresses several ways to resolve these problems: introduction of more direct democratic mechanisms, the protection of substantive democratic values through judicial review, and, more profoundly, inculcating democratic norms in the minds of both elites and ordinary citizens. Direct democratic mechanisms and judicial review alike can be understood as institutional efforts to get around the failure of representation. But, as discussed above, all institutional measures have their own limitations and certainly cannot be considered cure-alls. Without democratic norms that acknowledge democratic systems as the best and only game in town, and without an open and tolerant mindset that leads to treating others as equal members of the political community, institutional efforts alone can hardly bear fruit. In South Korea in particular, those institutional mechanisms have at best served as "speed bumps to slow the agglomeration and abuse of political power" (Bugarič 2019, 614), not as full remedies for the indicators of democratic backsliding. In addition, with regard to democratic norms, South Korea seems to be struggling with centralized party leadership that is too strong, as well as politically and socially polarized citizens, both of which seem to be regressing with respect to the spirits of tolerance and mutual respect.

Despite these developments, however, South Korea is fortunate to have such active and engaged citizens with so many aspirations for democracy. This is quite the opposite of what is found in many established democracies where support for democracy has been on the decline (Mounk 2018). A belief in democracy is important as it is the very ground on which our systems are built. After all, why should we bother to protect democracy when few believe in it? All the institutional and normative efforts discussed in this chapter are only meaningful when there is a popular consensus that democracy is the only game in town. In this regard, it can be said that in South Korea, procedural democracy and substantive democracy are not in contradiction. That is to say, engaging more people in the country's decision making is not likely to lead to a subversion of the democratic system.

To repeat, however, it would be premature to say that South Koreans, going beyond mere support for the system, have internalized more mature and substantive democratic values such as liberty and equality, accountability and representativeness, tolerance and protection for minority rights, and so on. We should not, therefore, hastily employ direct democratic measures for important political decisions; instead, we need to be patient and wait for citizens to develop such democratic norms and values. In the meantime, as one of the practical methods for cultivating such an active and respectful citizenship from the grassroots level, deliberative democracy has been attracting the attention of many scholars and policymakers in recent years (Jung 2020a).

Deliberative democracy is a type of democracy that uses wide and open public discussion as the key component of political decision-making (Bessette 1980; Dryzek 2000). It is often regarded as an alternative to both representative democracy and direct democracy as it seeks to allow for open and direct citizen participation as well as to foster informed and institutionalized discussion. It is thus, at least in theory, the best of both worlds (Jung 2020a). In South Korea, the concept of deliberative democracy was not so popular until the public deliberation committee on the construction of Shin-Gori nuclear reactors No. 5 and

6 was formed in 2017, ultimately providing its proposal on the basis of the final results of participatory surveys. Following this proposal, the Moon government decided to resume the construction of the reactors. A number of deliberative committees on a variety of policy issues have been structured since then, especially at the local level. South Korea's deliberative democracy is still at its rudimentary stages and is not without flaws (e.g., the discussion process is often swayed by those with stronger interests in the issue; Hong 2011). But, as the mechanism settles and takes root in grassroots politics, it is expected that deliberative democracy will complement the limitations of democratic representation, giving rise to a citizenry with mature democratic values.

Part II

Social Conflict and Inequality

04

Rising of Economic Inequality and Class Politics in South Korea

Jungsub Shin

Soongsil University

1. Introduction

Economic inequality is a significant social harm because it not only often directly causes social problems and conflicts, but also engenders other forms of inequality, e.g., political inequality (Stiglitz 2012). Therefore, severe economic inequality has been considered a great barrier to the development of democracy. In recent years, economic inequality has become a common problem for most democratic countries. As a new democracy that is going through democratic consolidation and a rapid economic development, South Korea is also facing rising economic inequality. The rising of economic inequality changed Korean politics as well as Korean perceptions about the economy and politics. This chapter examines how and why economic inequality has increased in South Korea, and how economic inequality affects Korean politics. Specifically, this chapter proceeds as follows. First, I examine how economic inequality has changed over time in South Korea, with a particular emphasis on income and assets inequality. Second, this chapter compares economic inequality in South Korea with that of other countries. Third, I discuss how worsening economic inequality in South Korea affects Korean citizens' attitudes and perceptions on life and politics.

2. Economic Inequality in South Korea

South Korea experienced a rapid compact growth after the Korean War. According to the Economic Statistics System of the Bank of Korea (ECOS), Gross National Income (GNI) per capita was $82 in 1959 and reached to $33,433 in 2018. According to ECOS, the average annual GNI growth of South Korea was 3.6% in the 1950s, but it rapidly increased throughout the 1960s to the 1980s. Average annual GNI growth was 10.4% in the 1960s, 22.8% in the 1970s, and 12.9% in the 1980s, though average annual GNI growth dropped to 6 % in the 1990s. The media and scholars have termed this phenomenon of rapid South Korean growth the 'Miracle on the Han River'. To be sure, such rapid economic growth is not without side effects and economic inequality is one of the most frequently experienced pains that rapidly developing countries encounter. Nevertheless, South Korea stayed a relatively equal country until the late 1990s (Koo 2007).

However, after the financial crisis of 1997, South Korea experienced unprecedented economic hardship, which led to great social and economic bipolarization and inequality (Koo 2007). Many large and small businesses collapsed and the unemployment rate skyrocketed. After the 1997 financial crisis, economic neoliberal reform was implemented by the Korean government under the guidance of the International Monetary Fund (IMF). This reform resulted in the very flexible labor market that engendered a greater proportion of precarious work (including an increase in non-regular workers) and deepened inequality and poverty

(Shin 2012). Although social security protection and programs expanded to absorb the shock of the economic neoliberal reform, the level of public social protection was not enough to cancel out the negative effects of the crisis and the following neoliberal reform (Kim et al. 2018).

Figure 4-1 shows how income inequality changed from 1990 to 2016 in South Korea. Presented are four GINI index[1] lines. The diamond line was calculated by market income of household samples that have more than two household members in cities (2HH_City). The square line was calculated by disposable income[2] of 2HH_City. The two lines show an almost identical curve. They increase to about 0.3 beginning in 1997 and continuously increase thereafter. Since 2006, ECOS has measured the GINI index by including all types of households. The triangle line shows the trends in the GINI index calculated using the market income of all types of households, and the X line calculated using the disposable income of all types of households. The triangle and X lines are higher than the diamond and the square lines, which means that income inequality among 2HH_City is lower than that among city households with only one-person and rural households.

When it comes to comparing the GINI index of market income with the GINI index of disposable income, the former is always higher than the latter. The implication is that government tax systems and social welfare programs have reduced income inequality in South Korea. The gap in the GINI index between market income and disposable income widens after 2009.

---

[1] Gini index measures the degree of inequality in the distribution of family income in a country. The more nearly equal a country's income distribution, the lower its Gini index. The range of GINI is 0 (perfect equality) to 1 (perfect inequality).

[2] Disposable income is income remaining after deduction of taxes and other mandatory charges, available to be spent or saved as one wishes.

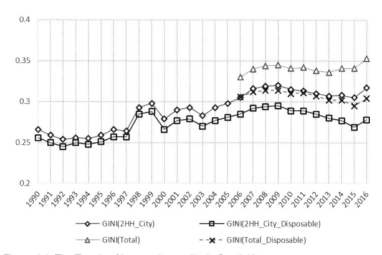

Figure 4-1. The Trends of Income Inequality in South Korea
Source: ECOS(Economic Statistic System of Bank of Korea) http://ecos.bok.or.kr/

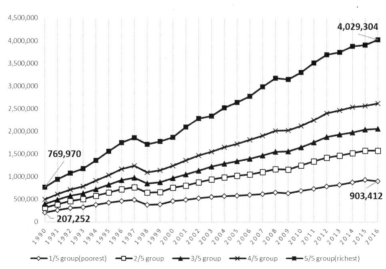

Figure 4-2. Monthly Disposable Income Growth in South Korea (in KRW)
Source: ECOS(Economic Statistic System of Bank of Korea) http://ecos.bok.or.kr/

Figure 4-2 presents more detailed information about how income inequality has changed in South Korea. It shows the trends of monthly disposable income growth of five income groups from 1990 to 2016. The households are divided into five groups from the richest (5/5 group) to the poorest (1/5 group) based on monthly income. The average income of the richest group (5/5 group) was about 769,970won and that of the poorest group (1/5 group) was 207,252 won in 1990. The average income of the richest group (5/5 group) is about 3.7 times that of the poorest group (1/5 group) in 1990. The income gap between the richest and the poorest groups has increased over 26 years. In 2016, the average income of the richest group (5/5 group) was about 4.5 times higher than that of the poorest group (1/5 group). Figure 4-2 indicates that the growth speeds of the four income groups from poorest to second richest (4/5 group) are very similar, and there is no large gap in income between the four groups. In contrast, the speed of income growth of the richest group is much faster than that of the other four groups. This implies that the rise of income inequality in South Korea is primarily caused by the income gap between the highest income group and the other income groups. In short, income inequality in South Korea increased after the 1997 financial crisis and never went back to the level prior to 1997, but it is also not a severe form of inequality except when considering the highest income group.

However, the real problem of economic inequality in South Korea is not with respect to income but with respect to assets. Figure 4-3 shows the change in asset growth among five asset-holding groups in South Korea.

Households are classified into five groups from the richest (5/5 group) to the poorest (1/5 group) according their household assets. As Piketty (2014) argues, asset inequality is much greater than income

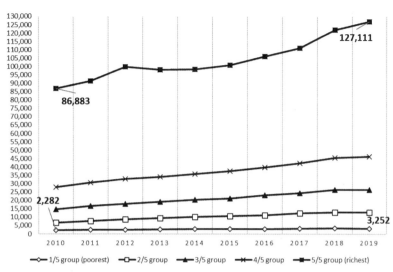

Figure 4-3. Household Assets Growth in South Korea (in 10,000 KRW)
Source: ECOS (Economic Statistic System of Bank of Korea) http://ecos.bok.or.kr/

inequality in many developed capitalist countries. Figure 4-3 demonstrates that this characterizes South Korea as well. The average assets of the richest group (5/5 group) was about 86 million won, while that of the poorest group (1/5 group) was about 23 million won in 2010. The average assets of the richest group (5/5 group) is therefore about 38 times greater than the poorest group (1/5 group) in 2010. The gap between the richest and the poorest groups has slightly increased over the last decade. In 2019, the average income of the richest group (5/5 group) was about 39 times higher than the poorest group (1/5 group). When comparing the income gap in 2016, average assets held by the richest group was about 1.6 billion won, while that held by the poorest group was about 30 million won in 2016. The assets of the richest group (5/5 group) were therefore about 35 times higher than those of the poorest group (1/5 group) in 2016. It is a much larger gap, especially compared to the income gap between the poorest and the richest in the same year (which stands at about 4.5 times). Today, therefore, asset inequality is much greater than income inequality in South Korea.

While I have thus far examined how economic inequality has changed over time in South Korea. Figures 4-4 and 4-5 show how economic inequality in South Korea compares to other OECD (Organization for Economic Cooperation and Development) countries in the lat-

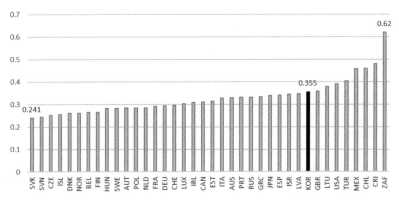

Figure 4-4. GINI Coefficient across OECD Countries (2017 or latest available)
Source: OECD (2020), Income inequality indicator. (doi: 10.1787/459aa7f1-en)

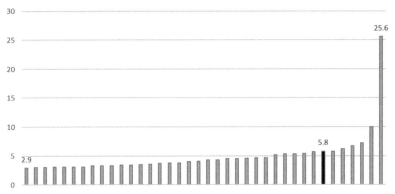

Figure 4-5. Interdecile P90/P10 Ratio across OECD Countries (2017 or latest available)
Source: OECD (2020), Income inequality indicator. (doi: 10.1787/459aa7f1-en)

est available year. Figure 4-4 presents GINI coefficients across OECD countries, illustrating that South Korea is ranked 9th worst. Figure 4-5 shows the interdecile P90/P10 Ratio across OECD Countries. P90/P10 is the ratio of the average income of the upper bound value of the ninth decile (i.e. the 10% of people with the highest incomes) to that of the first decile. That is, it is the ratio of the average income of the richest 10% to the poorest 10%. According to Figure 4-5, South Korea is ranked 7th worst P90/P10 Ratio among the 38 OECD countries.

Overall, economic inequality of South Korea in the last few years is very severe compared to other OECD countries. In the next section, this chapter will discuss how rising of economic inequality affects the attitudes and perceptions of Koreans with respect to politics.

3. The Consequence of Economic Inequality on Class Politics in South Korea

As mentioned above, there has been a dramatic change in economic inequality since the 1997 financial crisis in South Korea. The rapid increase in economic inequality has led to economic, social, and political changes. In particular, a social conflict between the haves and the have-nots has become severe. Consequently, class conflict has begun to affect the electoral decisions and political attitudes of Korean citizens over the last three decades.

In fact, class cleavages were historically not considered an important factor affecting vote choice in South Korea. After the 1987 Korean democratization, a regional cleavage tended to play a dominant role in Korean voting behavior (Choi 2006). Traditionally, Youngnam (southeastern provinces of South Korea) voters have voted mainly for parties on the right side of the political spectrum, while their Honam (southwestern provinces of South Korea) counterparts tended to support for parties on the left. Although other cleavages such as ideology and age have emerged as important determinants of vote choice (Kim et al. 2008), Korean voters have tended not to consider their class positions when making political choices.

Three reasons may account for the lack of a class-based politics in South Korea, even though the number of Korean working class increased tremendously during the rapid economic development period from the 1960s to the 1980s. Probably most importantly, class politics was repressed by authoritarian governments. Korea was divided after its independence from Japan in 1945. North Korea claimed itself as a communist country while South Korea pursued building a liberal democracy. The two Koreas then fought with each other from 1950 to 1953. This civil war made anti-communism the dominant ideology in South Korea after the Korean War. By using this political circumstance, Korean dictators such as President Chung-hee Park and President Doo-Hwan Chun suppressed labor movements or the political activities of laborers, regarding such activities as helping Communist North Korea (Choi 1988). Second, the rapid industrialization of South Korea from the 1960s to the 1980s brought economic growth with equity. During this period, the income of Korean households greatly improved without generally increasing income inequality (Leipziger et al. 1992), though there were some periodic fluctuations. Third, regionalism traditionally, overwhelmed electoral politics in South Korea. The repression of class politics began to ease off after the democratic transition of 1987, but regional cleavages appeared and dominated Korean electoral and party politics. Parties concentrated their efforts on mobilizing voters by building party-region linkages, while voters including workers casting their ballots for their preferred regional parties. The consequence was an absence of class politics and class voting.

However, economic inequality in South Korea has been growing markedly during the most recent 20 years of neoliberal reform. The 1997 financial crisis resulted in a radical neoliberal restructuring in Korea. Throughout this radical reform period, economic inequality both in terms of income and asset levels between the poor and the rich have rapidly increased (Kim 2017). Since then, despite steady economic growth, Koreans have experienced a severe worsening of economic equality in a sustained way for the first time. These trends have changed some attitudes and perceptions of Koreans toward Korean society. For example, according to the 2009 International Social Program Survey (ISSP) of Korea, more than 90% of Korean respondents mentioned that income gaps are very large and more than 70% mentioned that taxation levels for the higher income groups are too low. Also, Koreans have begun to exhibit a pessimistic perception of the possibility of social mobility.

Figure 4-6 shows the change of Korean perceptions about their child's upward social mobility over the last 25 years. Previous studies have argued that worsening economic inequality has caused most Koreans to think that Korea is quite unequal and that social mobility is very limited (Jung & Oh 2009; Kang 2012; Park & Suh 2012) due to the severe economic inequality deteriorating chances at education for the poor. Figure 4-6 shows evidence supporting this argument.

The percentage of respondents who said that their children will not fare better than them rapidly increased over time. In 1994, only 5.1 percent of respondents said 'low' regarding the predicted likelihood of their child's upward social mobility, but 55.5 percent answered similarly in 2019. Corak (2013) argued that education is one of the significant key factors for the poor or the lower classes to move to the middle class, but economic inequality in the parent generation often results in un-

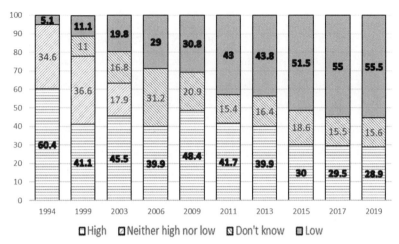

Figure 4-6. Expectation about Child's Upward Social Mobility

Note: The Question was asked to the household head like "What is your expectation on the chance that your children will fare better than you?" The answer choice set was changed after the 2006 Social Survey ('Neither high nor low' was removed from the answer set after the 2006 survey).

Source: Social Survey Series of Statistics Korea (http://kostat.go.kr/portal/eng/index.action)

equal educational opportunities or academic accomplishments in the generation that comes next. Therefore, worsening economic inequality leads people to have negative perceptions about upwards mobility in social status relative to their current social positions.

Under these circumstance, economic polarization sparked the conflict between the poor and the rich in Korea, a certain level of class consciousness arose among the working class and the poor (Kim et al. 2018). By analyzing original survey data from 2016, Kim et al. (2018) found that growing number of Korean citizens have a distinct class consciousness, with almost 40% of respondents having a very consistent and strong class consciousness. In particular, most respondents who have strong class consciousness also have pro-labor class consciousness. In addition, household assets, subjective social class perception, and occupations have significant impacts on whether a respondent has a strong and consistent class consciousness, though household income does not. This result implies that Koreans have begun to develop a class consciousness from the growing disparity between rich and poor, and this change would intensify political tensions in electoral politics in South Korea.

Therefore, it is not surprising that recent studies have found some evidence supporting the possibility of class voting.[3] For example, Kim (2010) Son (2010) and Lee et al. (2013) each found partial evidence that objective class positions influence vote choice. Kim (2010) analyzed microlevel survey data from the 2000 and 2004 Korean legislative elections and found that Korean voters vote according to their class positions. Son (2010) focused on economic assets like home ownership, especially apartment ownership,[4] and found that home ownership has a significant impact on the vote choices of Korean voters. Lee et al. (2013) also showed the possibility that household asset levels influence vote choice. In addition, Jang (2013) suggests the possibility that subjective class perceptions affect the voting choice.

There are still, however, several empirical studies arguing that there is no class voting at all in South Korea. Following the study of Kang (1998), Han (2013), Cheon & Shin (2014), and Moon (2017) all argue that there is no traditional connection between social class and party choice in South Korea. In contrast, these studies found that the poor and working class tend to support the conservative parties in Korean

---

[3] Class voting means that voting behavior among a given social class tends to support a particular political party (Evans 2017, 17). Traditionally, the working class or the poor vote for the left or the socialist party while the middle and upper classes vote for the right or conservative party (Lipset and Rokkan 1967).

[4] In Korea, an apartment is a popular type of houses that represent a class position (Son 2010).

elections. They call this the 'class betrayal vote'. According to these studies, a class cleavage has not yet been an important determinant of political choices for Korean voters in terms of the traditional meaning of class voting.

4. Conclusion

South Korea has experienced severe economic inequality since the 2000s. The 1997 financial crisis triggered liberal-economic reform as well as the severe economic inequality. However, major problems already existed as a result of the period of rapid economic development overseen by military dictators, which in turn eventually led to the recent rising economic inequality. Recent economic inequality in South Korea seems to be severe when compared to its own past and to the other OECD countries. In particular, asset inequality is much more severe than income inequality in South Korea. Although the Korean government has employed several social protection programs and increased social welfare spending, the economic inequality of South Korea yet keeps widening.

With growing economic inequality, the political and social attitudes of Koreans have changed as well. Trust in society deteriorated lower and pessimistic evaluations on life and society increased over the last 20 years (Cheon et al. 2013). In addition, the perception of Koreans on social mobility between generations has also grown increasingly pessimistic. In 2019, majority of Koreans thought that their children could not fare better than them. In terms of political attitudes, Koreans have grown increasingly aware of class. Although the percentage of Koreans who have class consciousness is smaller than that of western European countries, the number of people who are aware of class increases nowadays. Growing economic inequality and class consciousness in South

Korea have seemingly intensified class politics. According to the conventional wisdom, class cleavages were not one of the most important factors influencing vote choice in South Korea. However, recent studies on Korean voting behavior reported evidence supporting class voting, even though the argument that there is no class voting at all in South Korea persists.

05

The Advent of a Multicultural Society and Social Conflict in South Korea

Hoiok Jeong

Myongji University

As the number of foreigners living in Korea has been on the rise, the political and social influence of foreign residents and those from multicultural families is increasing. This political influence of demographic diversity is well represented in the 2005 revision of the Public Election Act. As a result of this amendment to the Public Election Act, foreigners aged 19 years or older have the right to vote in local elections three years after acquiring permanent residence in Korea (Lee 2011).

As such, the influence of democratic diversity has created new objectives for representative democracy, and their political influence is expected to increase further as the number of people targeted by these objectives gradually increases. Since the revision of the Public Election Act, the number of foreign electors has continually increased from the fourth local elections to the seventh local elections. The number of foreign electors, which was 6,726 in the fourth local election, increased to 12,878 in the fifth, 48,428 in the sixth, and 106,049 in the seventh.[1] In addition, the number of children of foreign residents aged 0 to 18 years old in Korea as of 2016 was 201,333.[2] These figures indicate that these children will become an important working-age population in Korea's future.

The increase in social diversity due to the influx of immigrants is expected to be a fundamental demographic change in Korean society. The aging of society due to a low birth rate will occur simultaneously with this transition to a multicultural society, which will accelerate the demographic diversity of Korea. In the past six decades, the aging index[3] has increased from 6.9 in 1960 to 67.2 in 2010, and it exceeded 110.5 in 2018.[4] The aging phenomena in Korea are not just the increase in average age but also the very noticeable acceleration of the aging process. Furthermore, the population growth rate in Korean society continues to decrease. Specifically, the growth rate of 0.76 in 2008 decreased to 0.37 by 2018.[5] The aging population and the decreasing population growth rate have led to a shrinking proportion of the population that is economically active, which causes an economic burden for the younger generation.

As the aging of Korean society escalates, the number of foreigners living in Korea continues to increase. The main reason for this phenomenon is the trend of globalization and its supply of manpower to some sectors of Korean society. Such demographic changes in Korean society and the resulting increase in social diversity are expected to increase the

---

1 http://www.nec.go.kr

2 https://www.mois.go.kr

3 The aging index indicates the ratio of the number of elderly persons of an age when they are generally economically inactive (aged 65 and over) to the number of young persons (from 0 to 14).

4 http://kostat.go.kr

5 http://kostat.go.kr

Table 5-1. 2015-2065 years the main national comparison

	Population growth rate			Age composition ratio						Total support ratio		
				2015			2065					
	15-20 years	35-40 years	60-65 years	0-14 years	15-64 years	65 years old +	0-14 years	15-64 years	65 years old +	Year 2015	2035 years	2065 years
South Korea	0.4	-0.2	-1.0	13.8	73.4	12.8	9.6	47.9	42.5	36.2	66.8	108.7
Greece	-0.2	-0.4	-0.7	14.6	64.0	21.4	12.1	53.0	34.9	56.2	66.1	88.6
Netherlands	0.3	0.0	-0.1	16.5	65.2	18.2	15.4	56.5	28.0	53.3	74.3	76.9
Norway	1.1	0.6	0.4	18.0	65.7	16.3	16.7	57.8	25.5	52.2	64.1	72.9
New Zealand	0.9	0.5	0.2	20.2	64.9	14.9	15.9	58.0	26.2	54.0	67.7	72.4
Denmark	0.4	0.2	0.2	16.9	64.2	19.0	16.3	57.7	26.1	55.9	69.2	73.3
Germany	-0.1	-0.3	-0.4	12.9	65.9	21.2	13.3	53.6	33.2	51.8	77.7	86.7
Mexico	1.2	0.6	-0.0	27.6	65.9	6.5	14.9	59.7	25.4	51.7	48.8	67.5
U.S.A	0.7	0.5	0.4	19.0	66.3	14.8	17.3	58.9	23.9	50.9	65.0	69.9
Belgium	0.6	0.2	0.1	16.9	64.8	18.2	16.0	56.8	27.2	54.2	68.8	76.1
Sweden	0.7	0.5	0.4	17.3	62.8	19.9	17.2	57.9	24.9	59.3	68.9	72.8
Swiss	0.8	0.4	0.2	14.8	67.2	18.0	15.3	55.7	29.1	48.8	68.8	79.6
Spain	0.0	-0.1	-0.5	14.9	66.3	18.8	12.7	53.8	33.6	50.8	68.3	86.0
England	0.6	0.4	0.2	17.8	64.5	17.8	16.2	57.6	26.2	55.1	66.5	73.6
Austria	0.3	0.0	-0.2	14.2	67.0	18.8	14.3	53.9	31.8	49.2	71.3	85.7
Italy	-0.0	-0.2	-0.4	13.7	63.9	22.4	13.3	52.9	33.8	56.5	78.4	89.1
Japan	-0.2	-0.6	-0.6	12.9	60.8	26.3	12.8	50.8	36.5	64.5	78.7	97.0
Czech Republic	0.1	-0.3	-0.4	15.0	66.9	18.1	14.6	55.5	29.9	49.5	59.9	80.1
Canada	0.9	0.5	0.3	16.0	67.9	16.1	15.1	56.8	28.0	47.3	66.1	75.9
Turkey	0.9	0.5	-0.0	25.7	66.8	7.5	15.1	59.3	25.6	49.7	49.6	68.7
Portugal	-0.4	-0.3	-0.6	14.1	65.2	20.8	11.7	53.1	35.2	53.5	69.1	88.4
Poland	-0.1	-0.6	-0.8	14.9	69.5	15.5	12.2	52.6	35.2	43.8	56.9	90.0
France	0.4	0.3	0.1	18.5	62.4	19.1	16.3	57.0	26.6	60.3	72.5	75.4
Australia	1.3	0.8	0.6	18.7	66.3	15.0	16.7	58.8	24.5	50.9	61.5	70.2

Source: Statistics Korea (www.kosis.kr), %, economically active population (hundred person)

political and social influence of multicultural populations and thereby lead to new changes and conflicts in the democratic political process.

How will demographic and social diversity change Korean society in the future? Population growth, which has slowed since 1965, is expected to fall into decline by 2065. In addition, the future population composition shows that the proportion of the population aged 65 or older will gradually increase, accounting for 42.5% of the total population in 2065. Meanwhile, the populations aged 0 to 14 years old and 15 to 64 years old are expected to decline. As of 2065, the population aged 0 to 14 years old is expected to account for 9.6% of the total population, and the population aged 15 to 64 years old will account for 47.9% of the total population.[6] In other words, the figure of the aging index of Korean society is expected to continue to increase. These combined issues mean Korean society will face enormous challenges in terms of demographics as the population's aging intensifies, the birth rate decreases, and the total population starts to decline.

Compared to other countries, the population's aging and the declining labor force population in Korea will become more serious. Table 5-1 shows the population growth rate, age composition ratio, and total support ratio of various countries from 2015 to 2065. According to the table, Korea's population growth rate in 2065 (-1.0) will be the lowest, and its proportion of people aged 65 and over in 2065 (42.5) will be the highest. The total support ratio in 2065 is also projected to be the highest, at 108.7, compared to the other countries examined.

As the demographic composition of Korean society changes and the importance of the multicultural populations that brought about this change increases, these populations' political influence is bound

---

6 http://kostat.go.kr

to increase. Therefore, the issue of their political representation will continue to be raised in social discourse, and thus politicians are likely to present more policies and commitments aimed at better representing multicultural populations. Political parties and politicians will also be pressured to be more proactive in enacting policies and legislation to accommodate migrants. In addition, multicultural groups will be influential in the political process of Korea by forming their own political parties and interest groups to represent their interests through the process of organizing and empowering.

Alongside the demographic change and the progress of social diversity in Korean society, a change in Koreans' perceptions and attitudes toward those multicultural groups might occur. Koreans' perceptions of multiculturalism are currently positive in terms of the economy, but there is also a reluctance to support multiculturalism among Koreans who seem afraid of increased crime rates due to immigrants. In a poll that asked Koreans about immigrants,[7] 53.0% of the respondents agreed with the statement that immigrants increase the crime rate, while 35.2% did not agree. However, when asked about immigrants' contributions to social and economic development, the positive responses were much higher, with 53.2% agreeing that immigrants contribute to social development and 63.2% agreeing that they contribute to economic development. In addition, 44.5% said that support for immigrants was not excessive, while 67.7% said Korea should block illegal immigrants.

In short, many Koreans tend to see immigrant groups as acceptable for the purpose of economic development. However, Koreans tend to lack the willingness to recognize them as members of the same com-

---

[7] The Asian Institute for Policy studies (http://www.asaninst.org)

munity, as seen in Koreans' negative attitudes, such as concerns that immigrants will increase crime rates in Korean society. Relatedly, the issue of refugee acceptance shows possible conflict among Korean society when faced with demographic diversity. According to the report,[8] only 37.4% said they would accept refugees, but 53.4% said they would not accept them.

The findings that many Korean citizens have negative perceptions of the transformation of Korean society into a multicultural society, witnessed in cases such as immigration and refugee acceptance, are likely to affect the development of social diversity in Korean society in the future. In other words, as social diversity increases, there is a strong possibility that conflicts in Korean society will increase and social integration will deteriorate. When considering this possibility, it is necessary to discuss not only what influences natives' attitudes toward immigration but also what affects immigrants' attitudes toward their host country.

First, taking a look at the literature on natives' attitudes toward immigration,[9] it should be noted that the issue of immigration is closely related to the notions of country or nation. Opinions toward immigrants begin from the issue of whether one will allow out-group members into his or her group. This implies that immigration issues are inseparable from the notion of identity toward one's own nation or country. Therefore, it is important to clarify what national identity means in order to have a deep understanding of one's attitudes toward immigration. According to the previous literature, national identity is defined as the sense of belonging to the country that one shares with

---

[8] https://www.realmeter.net

[9] Some part of the following literature review was taken from my article, Do National *Feelings Influence Public Attitudes towards Immigration?* (Journal of Ethnic and Migration Studies, 2013).

fellow citizens and as the beliefs of individuals in relation to their countries (Hjerm 2005; Yun and Song 2011). National identity provokes attitudes of inclusion toward those that one identifies as belonging to his or her nation, and attitudes of exclusion toward immigrants who are perceived as being members of an out-group (Hjerm 1998).

National identity, however, does not take one single form. Indeed, it is often considered to have two forms: either ethnic-genealogical or civic-territorial (Smith 1991; Jones and Smith 2001). Ethnic identity focuses collective memories as a group sharing a common destiny. It emphasizes characteristics, such as people being the descendants of the same ancestors and sharing cultural heritages and traditions. Therefore, ethnic identity has strong ascriptive attributes highlighting lineage more important than territories, customs, and systems. Civic identity clearly differs from ethnic identity. Civic identity considers qualifications related to territories and political communities to be more important for becoming members of the country. Thus, it can be said that civic identity has strong selective and voluntary attributes. Furthermore, civic identity tends to focus on the observance of systems and customs as citizens and the exercise of the rights and obligations (Jones and Smith 2001; Choi 2007).

Why would national identity have an impact on how people perceive immigration and immigrants? The answer to this question relies on the theory of symbolic politics. Symbolic politics theory argues for the important role of symbolic concerns when individuals form attitudes on certain issues. The theory maintains that people care about abstract political symbols, even though the emotional costs they pay and the benefits that they receive from such involvements are modest (Sears 1993). According to Sears (1993), people acquire stable affective responses to particular symbols through a process of classical conditioning. These learned dispositions might not continue through one's adult life, but the strongest do. The strongest dispositions are called "symbolic predispositions" (Sears 1993). National identity is one of the most important symbolic concerns that individuals use to perceive the political world and make political decisions.

Turning to what influences immigrants' attitudes toward host society,[10] one of the most pressing concerns in societies with an increasing number of immigrants is ensuring that migrants have a safe level of trust in mainstream political institutions. There are two main perspectives from which to explain immigrants' political trust and integration into the host country. First, some studies emphasize that immigrant assimilation is the key to promoting attachment to political institutions in a host country. This perspective, called "straight line assimilation" or "classic assimilation," argues that as immigrants spend more time in a host country and identify with its society, they are more likely to have positive attitudes about mainstream institutions (Alba and Nee 2003; Gordon 1964; Joppke and Morawska 2003). In other words, immigrants often face initial integration difficulties, but over time, their life outcomes converge with those of native people. And with sufficient time in a host country, immigrants will successfully integrate. The key mechanisms that facilitate this process are the acquisition of citizenship and the gradual adoption of the host society's language and culture (Park, Burgess, and Mckenzie 1925; Gordon 1964). The perspective of straight line assimilation predicts that cultural and social assimilation would precede attitudinal assimilation, which would precede the absence of prejudice and discrimination (Maxwell 2008). The logic

---

10 This part was adapted from my article, *A New Typology of Perceived Discrimination and Its Relationship to Immigrants' Political Trust* (Polish Sociological Review, 2016).

behind this claim is that, as immigrants become culturally and socially like the native people of a country, they will adopt native attitudes, which will give natives fewer incentives to discriminate against immigrants (Maxwell 2008).

However, this prediction misses an important fact of reality, which is that immigrants are generally viewed as cultural outsiders and tend to be stigmatized as inassimilable groups who are subject to discrimination. Thus, another point of view on immigrants' political trust and integration, often called "segmented assimilation" in the literature, receives support. The second perspective focuses on the barriers to assimilation that many minority immigrants face. These arguments illustrate how entrenched socio-economic difficulties, stigmatization, and discrimination alienate immigrants from mainstream institutions (Howell and Fagan 1988; Schildkraut 2005). Thus, assimilation is not always a smooth and unidirectional process (Safi 2010) and is not only a matter of time. The host society plays an important role in the process through mechanisms of discrimination against immigrant groups. The hostility immigrants experience in the receiving society associates a psychological cost with their political attitudes. Discrimination creates social, economic, and political problems for integration and may eventually lead immigrants to become distrustful with and alienated from mainstream society (Waters 1999; Portes, Fernández-Kelly, and Haller 2005). That is, a focus on discrimination attracts attention to the attitudes of the host society as an important factor in the immigrant's assimilation process (Safi 2010).

Based on the segmented assimilation literature, the driving force behind immigrants' feelings of trust in political institutions might be their perceptions of discrimination. The evaluation of the performance of political institutions has both instrumental and relational aspects to it (Newton and Norris 2000; Mishler and Rose 2005; Roder and Muhlau 2011). When in direct contact with institutions, citizens read the way they are treated as signals of their valuation as members of the society, and procedural fairness concerns become salient in their judgment (Tyler 2006). A more important, although frequently neglected, aspect of institutional performance is the capacity to create a fair and inclusive society. "Fairness-generating institutions" "must enshrine concepts such as fairness, justice, incorruptibility, non-partisanship, truthfulness, or even transparency as the core norms of communal living,... they are universally oriented and provide their citizens with equal opportunities" (Freitag and Bühlmann 2009; 8-9). Thus, Safi (2010) maintains that discrimination explains the disparities in many aspects of political attitudes, including life satisfaction, between immigrants and natives. The experience of discrimination by third parties influences trust in political institutions, as immigrants may feel that political institutions fail in their responsibilities if they do not prevent these acts of discrimination by third parties (e.g., Kääriäinen 2007: Röder and Muhlau 2011).

However, the segmented assimilation literature is not without its problems. It uncritically assumes the uni-dimensionality of the perceived discrimination of immigrants. Far fewer studies have examined the multi-dimensional character of perceived discrimination and its impact on political trust among immigrants. Most studies tend to regard perceptions of discrimination as having only one aspect and empirically focus on only one questionnaire item that asks "whether or not the respondent belongs to a group which is discriminated against in society" or combines all questions on discrimination (e.g., Röder and Mühlau 2011; Maxwell 2008; 2010; Michelson 2003). It obscures the true impact of perceived discrimination on political trust. This neglect is unfortunate because individuals feel discriminated against for various reasons. For instance, some might feel that they are being discriminated against because of their ethnicity, while others might feel discriminated against because of their religion, and still others may feel discriminated against because of their gender or age. These reasons for discrimination might include nationality, language, ethnicity, race, religion, age, gender, disability, and so on.

In addition, it is important to consider how migrants' political trust is shaped by immigration status. The mechanisms underlying the formation of political trust are not similar across generations. More specifically, the impact of perceptions of discrimination on political trust from second-generation immigrants might demonstrate different patterns from those same perceptions among first-generation immigrants, which means that the perceptions of second-generation immigrants are similar to those of native people. This might be because second-generation immigrants have grown up in the same environment as native-origin individuals and are likely to share a similar experience with and evaluations of the host society. For instance, Röder and Mühlau (2011) claim that children of immigrants born in the country of residence have little or no contact with the home country of their parents and are likely to take their lead from their peers rather than their parents.

In conclusion, South Korea is on the road to becoming a multicultural society, with the possibility of social conflict occurring. To decrease the intensity of social conflict and increase social integration, it is vital to discuss what determines native Koreans' attitudes toward immigrants and what influences immigrants' opinions toward mainstream Korean society. With these two sides considered, we will be able to formulate policies and social programs to better prepare for the advent of a multicultural society.

06

Generational Conflicts in Korea

Euisuok Han

Sungshin Women's University

1. Introduction

Generational conflict has been noted as a major social conflict in current Korean society since at least the 2000s. Specifically, presidential and general elections in the early 2000s raised the discourse on generation as a cleavage, and the media and academia began to consider generational conflict an important issue in Korean politics and society. Meanwhile, the concept and definition of a generation and its presence became a topic of academic debates due to its conceptual vagueness and difficulties in measurement. A generation can be defined as a group of people who were born in the same period and experienced the same socio-political events, having common consciousness. But sociologists argue that this 'cohort effect' is not enough for understanding the characteristics of a generation. Therefore, we should simultaneously consider the effects of aging and period (Park 2001). Among these effects, the cohort effect is linked to the common experiences shared by the same generation, while the aging effect is linked to the biological and social processes of aging. The period effect, on the other hand, occurs because of specific events that affect all generations at the same time. Distinguishing those three effects in a generation study is important for scientific research, but this chapter does not take up that task. Instead, it deals with the differences among generations in terms of ideology and policy preferences, and introduces socio-political discourses on generational cleavages in Korean society, in the name of 'generational conflicts.'

Critics of the discourse on generational conflict point out that the level of generational conflict has been exaggerated by the media and manipulated by political actors. Hence, they argue that discourses on generational conflict are overproduced and generational conflicts have no social reality. The argument contains a partial truth, however: generational conflict and intergenerational differences (gap) have become widely perceived and identified as one of the major social conflicts in Korea, alongside regional, class, and ideological conflict. Actually, it is plausible that the media and political mobilization by parties strengthened perceptions of generational conflicts, but the perceived conflicts re-construct Korean society and affect voters' choice in elections (Lee 2018, 21).

A survey on social conflicts in 2016 shows that 59.6% of respondents answered that generational conflict is one of the most serious social conflicts in Korea, next to class conflict, ideological conflict, and labor-management conflict (KIHASA 2018, 76). Moreover, the amount of coverage in newspapers about generational conflict rapidly increased in the 2010s, and it was more than double the news coverage for class and gender conflicts (KIHASA 2018, 40; 47). An analysis of newspaper articles from 2000 to 2013 reveals that articles on generation rapidly increased from 2010. Among those articles, 55.5% dealt with the relationship between economic issues and generation, while socio-cultural topics were 15.2%, politics 14.8%, and family issues 14.4% (KEDI 2015). That is, generational conflicts are prominent in the economic sphere. In addition to economic issues, generational conflicts include a variety of aspects (e.g., political, ideological or cultural conflicts among generations), and the conflicts often evolve into a struggle for power and social values. According to theories of generational conflict, those conflicts are primarily caused by four factors: different points of view resulting from the absence of common historical experiences, economic confrontation resulting from economic hardship, politico-ideational difference, and a lack of communication among generations (Sohn et al. 2019). While studies of generational conflict in Korea in the 2000s focused on differences between the so-called 'industrialization generation' and 'democratization generation' in politics, studies of generational conflict in the 2010s emphasize economic competition between younger and older generations. All these conflicts reflect power struggle, ideological difference and policy preference for the distribution of political and economic resources among generations.

2. Generational conflicts in politics

Elections and generational conflicts

Different voting pattern among the different generations were substantial in the Korean presidential election of 2002. Elections since democratization in 1987 have been influenced mainly by regional cleavages between Kyongsang province (Youngnam; Southeast Korea) and Cholla province (Honam; Southwest Korea). People from or living in each region have shown strong voting loyalty to political leaders and parties that have local ties with their hometowns. However, the generation factor worked in the 2002 presidential election when Roh Moo-Hyun and Lee Hoe-Chang competed for the presidency. A considerable number of voters in their 20s and 30s supported Roh as a liberal candidate, but voters in their 50s and 60s preferred the conservative Lee. The election raised a generational cleavage issue in Korean politics, although regionalism was still a major factor of electoral choice for Korean voters. When President Roh was elected, the so called '386 generation', who were in their 30s, entering university in the 1980s, born in the 1960s, was noted as a leading political force who supported a non-mainstream politician Roh Moo-Hyun. Further, many politicians from the 386 generation served as government officials during the Roh presidency. When the 386 generation became older, people began to refer them as 'the 86 generation' after they reached their 40s and 50s. Naming specific generations is controversial, but several generation-names have been widely used in Korea. At first, there was 'the industrialization generation,' who were born in the 1940s and the 1950s and experienced rapid economic growth. The 386 generation, who were born in the 1960s and experienced democratization in their 20s can be referred to as 'the democratization generation' at the same time. The term, '88 man-won generation,' which reflects the economic difficulties experienced by the younger generations, became popular when a book titled '88 man-won generation' was published in 2007. The word connotes the low incomes and economically unfair conditions for the youth (in their 20s), caused by neoliberal economic reforms since the late 1990s.

According to analyses of the 2007 presidential election and the 2008 national assembly election, the impact of generational cleavages was relatively weak. But the 2012 presidential election was different in the sense that changes in the Korean population structure could have been a significant variable in the election due to the increase numbers of older Korean voters. An increase in voters in their 50s and 60s who prefer conservative values and policies, and their majority support for candidate Park Geun-Hye was a crucial factor in her election as president (Lee and Chung 2013, 39). The national population census shows that the number of people in their 50s and 60s increased from 16.27% in 2000 to 22.0% in 2010, while those in their 20s and 30s decreased from 35.28% to 29.98% over the ten years. The rate of the population aged from their 50s to their 70s, who may prefer a conservative politician, increased from 19.6% to 27.5% during the same period.[1]

Results of presidential elections in 2002 and 2012 clearly present evidence in favor of the idea that generational cleavages worked in the Korean elections. Figure 6-1 illustrates the contrast between the younger generation's preference for a progressive ticket, Roh Moo-Hyun and Moon Jae-In, and the older generation's preference for conservatives Lee Hoe-Change and Park Geun-Hye.

As seen in the below figures, progressive presidential ticket Roh and Moon gained more votes from the younger generations, while conservative ticket Lee and Park obtained more votes from the older generations. Generational cleavage in electoral politics clearly appeared in both elections. Among those electoral results, the choice by the cohort in their 50s in 2012 is the most interesting. While majority of voters in their 50s preferred conservative candidate Park Geun-Hye in the 2012 election, their preference for conservative and progressive candidates was about half and half when they were in their 40s. It is inferred, then, that as the generation in their 40s in 2002 became older, more people in the same generation (in their 50s in 2012) shifted their politico-

---

[1] http://kosis.kr/index/index.do

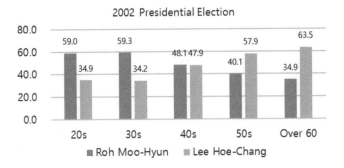

2002 Presidential Election

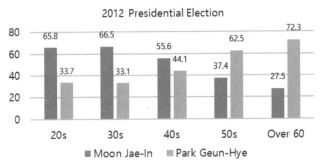

2012 Presidential Election

Figure 6-1. Voting Turnout in Presidential Elections of 2002 and 2012 by Age (%)
Source: Exit Poll by MBC, KBS and SBS
   http://weekly.khan.co.kr/khnm.html?artid=201212242003551&mode=view

ideational orientation into conservative ideology and policies. Discourse on the 386 generation in 2002 and electoral results in 2002 and 2012 present that the generational difference in Korean society came from an aging effect as well as a cohort effect. That is, the cohort and aging effects can be mingled and work at the same time.

Political issues in generational conflicts: North Korea

Policies regarding North Korea have been hot issues in South Korean politics, reflecting ideological conflicts between the younger and older generations, as well as between progressives and conservatives. In many cases, ideological cleavages overlap with generational cleavages between younger and older groups (Song and Lee 2019, 120). That is, the older generation tends to take a hawkish position against North Korea, while the younger generation takes a dovish position. But it does not mean all individuals within the younger (or older) generations share the same perceptions and attitudes toward the issue of North Korea. A survey conducted after the 2018 United States-North Korea summit in Singapore, showed that generational cleavages regarding the question of how to handle North Korea are more complicated.

Table 6-1 shows that South Korean in their 20s have more conservative attitudes toward North Korea and its leader Kim Jong-Un, illustrating more negative perceptions of North Korea among this young cohort than the perceptions of those over the age of 60. This implies that the current generation in their 20s has very conservative perspective on national security issues (Kim et al. 2018, 22). By contrast, respondents in their 40s and 50s (overlapped with the 386 generation) exhibited relatively positive perceptions regarding North Korea and its leader. Similarly, the generation in their 20s evaluated the 2018 North Korea-United States summit relatively negatively. 65.4% of respondents in their 20s evaluated the summit positively, while 82.5% of respon-

Table 6-1. Image on North Korea and its leader Kim Jong-Un

Age (generation)	North Korea	Kim Jong-Un
20s	**3.95**	**3.00**
30s	4.88	4.05
40s	**5.45**	**5.06**
50s	5.09	4.42
Over 60	4.20	3.71
Average	**4.71**	**4.06**

Note: Unit: 0 to 10 (from negative to positive)
Source: ASAN Report "North Korea-United States Summit and the South Korean Perception of Neighboring Countries" (July 2018).

dents in their 40s viewed it positively (Kim et al. 2018, 14).

According to a survey on perceptions about forming a joint women's ice hockey team, conducted ahead of the 2018 Pyeongchang Winter Olympic games, 72.2% of respondents answered that they were opposed to building a North-South joint women's ice hockey team, although 81.2% of them supported North Korea's participation in the Olympics (Koreatimes May 1, 2018).[2] It was interesting in that South Korean youth expressed strong animosity toward a 'one-team Korea' at that time. This incident could be related to indifference to the unification of Korea. A report by the Korea Institute for National Unification in July of 2017 revealed that only 20.5% of South Korean in their 20s supported unification of Korea, while 47.3% of people over 60 supported it (Korea Joongang Daily Jan 20, 2018).[3] Moreover, the primary reason for the opposition among those in their 20s to the joint team was a feeling of 'unfairness' because several members of the South Korean women's ice hockey team would certainly lose their chance to play in the Olympics. Criticism against the one-team Korea among younger generations also related to their economic difficulties. The younger generation has been suffering from economic hardships, such as a lack of job opportunities and discrimination in the wage payment system under Korea's neoliberal economic system and low economic growth. As a result, a feeling of relative deprivation and generational inequity has become a significant factor in the younger generation's perspective on socio-economic issues, bringing about a request for fairness and social justice. It is possible that the opposition among those in their 20s to the joint women's ice hockey team may not be proof of their ideologi-

---

2 https://www.koreatimes.co.kr/www/nation/2018/05/103_248242.html

3 http://koreajoongangdaily.joins.com/news/article/article.aspx?aid=3043546

cal orientation as conservatives (The Hankyoreh August 19, 2018).4 We should understand that the term 'ideology' has multidimensional meanings for each generation. For Korea's older generation, ideology connotes an attitude toward North Korea and anti-communism. But for the younger generation, it may involve a position on economic growth and redistribution instead of a policy position toward North Korea (Yun and Rhee 2014, 289). In this sense, the generation in their 20s may not necessarily be considered conservative, and we need to observe generational differences in Korea carefully.

3. Generational conflicts in economy

Research about generational cleavages between younger and older generations revealed that they have a considerable difference of perception on economic growth and redistribution, economic democratization, and welfare policies as well as a relationship with North Korea (KIHASA 2018, 161). As the research pointed out, generational conflicts in the 2010s have intensified in the economic sphere, as seen in Table 6-2. Specifically, generational conflicts in the 2010s involve economic issues including jobs, wages, and employment. Although the economic status of the younger generation is multilayered within the

Table 6-2. Analysis of Keywords about Generational Conflicts in Newspaper Articles

	Keywords about Generational Conflicts
1990s	inter-class, regionalism, democratization, inter-region, youth
2000s	people, economic disparity, political circles, the aged, democratization
2010s	jobs, polarization, retirement age extension, Korea, wage peak system

Source: KIHASA (2018, 41) Table 2-2.

---

4 http://english.hani.co.kr/arti/english_edition/e_northkorea/858228.html

same generation, the generation shares dissatisfaction with the vested economic interests of the older generations (Lee and Jang 2015, 16).

An increase in generational conflicts in the economic sphere reflects changes in Korean society in the 2000s and after. Neoliberal reforms after the 1997 financial crisis resulted in harsh competition in the labor market and an increase in non-regular jobs. Furthermore, growth of the aged population and a low birth rate brought about disputes regarding the pension system and generational inequity.

Since neoliberal economic globalization and consequent neoliberal reforms in the 2000s, discrimination against non-regular jobs has intensified. For example, the average wage of non-regular workers decreased from 67.1% of the average wage of regular workers to 54.6% of regular workers' wages between 2002 and 2018 (KOSIS 2019).[5] It was more unfavorable for workers in their 20s, because the rate of employees in non-regular jobs for people in their 20s is higher when compared to that of other generations. Meanwhile, a strong seniority system in Korean companies leads to a wage disadvantage to the younger generation too. Compared to the average wage of one-year newcomers in workplaces hiring over 10 regular employees, that of thirty-year veteran workers was 3.11 times higher in 2017 (The Dong-A Ilbo December 26, 2018).[6] The wage gap was even wider than that of Japan (2.37 times) and almost double that of the EU. Passage of the Retirement Age Extension Act in 2013, taking effect in 2016, might be perceived as a threat to the younger generation. The law revised the obligatory retirement age of employees, which employers guarantee, as 60. This could lead to shrinking job opportunities for the younger generation.

---

[5] Korean Statistical Information Service. https://mn.kbs.co.kr/news/view.do?ncd=4182804
[6] http://www.donga.com/news/article/all/20181225/93441867/1

These unfavorable labor conditions for the younger generation raise a generational inequality issue as well. Furthermore, the unemployment rate among people in their 20s was much higher than that of the other generations. Their unemployment rate was 9.0% while that of people in their 60s was 4.8% in February of 2020 (KOSIS 2020).

As mentioned above, generational differences or cleavages in Korea lead to a struggle for political power and economic gains. In addition, generational differences in social values and culture, as well as within family, may result in conflicts among generations. However, there are many critics who cast doubt on the utility and reality of the concept of 'generational conflicts.' They have argued that generational conflicts have been exaggerated and used for political and commercial benefit. Moreover, generational conflicts are used to conceal class conflict as the real underlying cause of social conflicts. Sociologist Chun Sangchin describes this as 'generation game,' in which power elites attempt to mobilize supporters for their political advantages, or avoid blame on them, making someone else a scapegoat (2018, 28). When the Park Geun-Hye administration launched pension reform and labor reform including a wage peak system, the government exploited generational conflicts as a strategy to carry out its policy goals. The government argued that reform of the pension system and the introduction of the wage peak system are necessary not to place an unfair burden on the younger generation, because the older generation has taken advantage of the present pension and wage systems at the cost of the younger generation (Cho and Kim 2016). From this perspective, a book published in 2019, *The Generation of Inequality*, written by Cheol-Sung Lee, is remarkable in that he argues the 386 generation (now known as 'the 586 generation' because the generation aged into their 50s) is a major actor in building economic inequalities within Korean society. He argues that the current younger generation is a victim of an unequal structure made from a combination of generation network (especially the 586 generation) and a hierarchical structure.

Generational differences, or generational cleavages, cannot turn into a social conflict or power struggle by themselves. So does social class and class cleavage. In this sense, political mobilization and identity-building by socio-political actors and media would be important. Besides, structural changes that lead to self-awareness as a generation may transform generational identity into generational conflict. When there is a political opportunity, generational differences or cleavages turn into generational conflict and go into a battlefield for values and interests. Table 6-3 shows why and by whom generational conflicts happen. Discourse on generational conflicts could be exaggerated and politically constructed. However, as a factor underlying social conflicts, generational conflicts are receiving increased attention in South Korea.

Currently, demographic change raises debates about the possibility of a gerontocracy or silver democracy. For example, the percentage of the population over the age of 60 became 25.68% among those over the age of 20 in 2018, while the percentage was 20.69% in 2010 (KOSIS

Table 6-3. Structure and Actors of Generational Conflicts

	Element	Causes
Structure	Economic condition: recession, low growth	Generational inequality and equity in distribution measures due to a lack of resources
	Demographic change: aging society, low birth rate	
Actors	Political parties	Political mobilization
	Businesses	Profit creation
	Media	Struggles over discourse
	Intellectuals	

Source: Table 1 in Lee and Jang (2015, 21). Revised by the author.

2020). That is, almost a quarter of all voters in Korea crossed over the age of 60 in 2018 (the voting age in South Korea was lowered to 18 in 2020). Moreover, voter turnout among the older generation has been relatively high compared to that of the younger generation. In the 2016 general election, for example, turnout rates among those in their 60s and 70s were 71.7% and 73.3%, while turnout among those in their 20s and 30s were 52.7% and 50.5%.[7] This means that the older generation can be a dominant actor in the policy-making process because parties and politicians would promise and make policies for the aged to attract their votes. Whether a gerontocracy or silver democracy will be realized in the near future is very controversial, but it reflects the fear of concentration of power by the older generation. Regardless of the feasibility of a gerontocracy, an increase in the discourse on power dominance by the aged presents a situation in which generational conflicts will continue to be a major source of political conflict in Korea as well as other industrialized countries.

4. Summary

Some critics argue that the level of generational conflict and its impact on society have been exaggerated and that regarding a generation as a homogeneous group may lead to a misunderstanding about generational conflicts. In fact, it is difficult to find a commonly shared ideology or political orientation within a generation. However, like nationalism or religion, generation can be a unit of identity that binds members of a generation together; that is, when generation meets a specific political opportunity and someone mobilizes it. Hence, politicization of generational conflicts can happen any time, simply due to the

---

[7] https://www.nec.go.kr

normal incentive structure.

We have observed that politicians have used discourses on generation in elections, government officials have used it in policy-making,
and intellectuals have approached social conflicts from a generational
conflict perspective. Meanwhile, patterns of generational conflicts in
Korea show that generational conflicts intensified in politics during the
2000s and in the economic sphere during 2010s, reflecting democratization, globalization and neo-liberalization. All of these facts point to
the idea that generational conflicts are a real problem in Korean society
and politics. But alleviating generational conflict will not be an easy
task because the conflict, mixed with other sources of social conflicts
such as ideological conflict, are in turn mixed with interests and values
as elements of the conflict themselves. Therefore, we should continue to
identify the main causes of generational conflict and find ways to ease
it, if possible.

Part III

Social Inclusion and Political Tolerance

07

Political Tolerance in Korea

Sung-jin Yoo

Ewha Womans University

1. Political Tolerance and Democracy

In principle, democracy is based on two fundamental values for individuals: liberty and equality. As a result, any individual is free to express his or her voice in a democratic society. Freedoms of speech and association, the rights of citizens to vote, demonstrate publicly, and hold an elected political office are necessary for any society to be democratic. Political tolerance, defined as the willingness to grant political rights to any member of society, is central to studies of democratic values, given its link with civil liberties and political freedoms (Lawrence 1976, 85). Members of democratic societies are educated to acknowledge and respect people with different opinions. Political tolerance requires that any people living in a democracy should be guaranteed political rights, regardless of age, sex, race, social position, or opinion.

Even though they are seemingly evident, such fundamental principles are often the basis of problems in democratic societies. Any community, even democratic ones, is composed of individuals and groups with different interests and preferences. Naturally, such differences give rise to conflict among people living in democracies. If the conflict becomes severe, it may lead to hatred among peopleand, sometimes, prejudice toward others. When such hatred and prejudice toward specific groups are prevalent in society, people become reluctant to acknowledge the rights of target groups. It is no wonder that the seminal work on political tolerance began with the phenomenon of how the public viewed the civil liberties of disliked groups (Stouffer 1955).

In the accumulated works on political tolerance, the most significant finding is that establishing and maintaining tolerant public remains a challenge. Nontrivial gaps between tolerance in principle and in practice remain in both established and nascent democracies (Marquart-Pyatt and Paxton 2007). If society fails to maintain the level of political tolerance to some degree, it may lead to the collapse of democracy because some citizens may be denied their political rights, and eventually excluded from democratic practices of the society altogetherarticipation altogether. All in all, maintaining a tolerant public is a requirement for any society to be considered democratic.

This chapter aims to investigate changes and continuities in political tolerance in South Korea. South Korea is known as one of the new democracies achieving political democratization as well as economic prosperity. Still, as a divided country, it remains heavily influenced by the legacy of the Cold War. Severe ideological conflict persists due to the tension between two Koreas. Furthermore, as Korea becomes more of a multicultural community, it is no longer free, as it wasin the past, from persistent challenges in advanced democracies such as the controversies of immigrants and LBGT . Citizens in Korea need to deal with multicultural issues and learn how to live with new members of society.

New and old issues suggest that we should not wait any longer to address political tolerance in Korea. The next section identifies the object and the current state of political tolerance in the context of Korea. Who are citizens tolerant of in Korea? Which political rights are granted to them? Then, I briefly look over the trend of political tolerance in Korea by examining attitudes toward political minorities with relevant survey data. Finally, I conclude this chapter by discussing the meaning of political tolerance in the era of political polarization.

2. Political Tolerance in the Korean Context

While in some contexts tolerance toward specific groups has fluctuated and may have even attenuated, it is possible that levels of tolerance have remained the same or even increased in other contexts (Gibson 2008; 2013; Shafer and Shaw 2009; Sullivan and Hendriks 2009). In addition, threat and economic downturn may lead to shifts in attitudes toward granting the government authority to suspend civil liberties, as was observed in the United States following the 9/11 terrorist attacks (Davis 2007; Huddy et al. 2005; Sullivan and Hendriks 2009). Although a growing number of studies attest to the importance of investigating tolerance worldwide, research reveals it to be contextually grounded, as well as potentially developing at uneven rates globally, leading to complexities regarding how it is realized locally, nationally, and globally.

South Korea is not an exception. As a well-known single-ethnic country, there has been little academic interest in political tolerance toward social minority groups in Korea. Unlike other democratic countries with ethnic and racial minorities, there were few groups in Korea whose members had been discriminated against, and those groups that have been discriminated against have relatively few members. Nevertheless, there was one specific group not welcomed by Korean society: communists. The Korean war established two completely different political regimes on the Korean peninsula. In South Korea, communists have always been under severe surveillance, and political norms prohibit citizens from helping or even supporting communists. If anyone were identified as communist even now, he or she would be punished by law. Under the military regimes in the 1970s and 1980s, communists were a target of punishment. It is thus not debatable whether communists are granted political rights.

The political democratization of 1987 and the collapse of communism led to a new phase of political tolerance in Korea. South Korea normalized relationships with former communist countries, including Russia and east European countries. Communism is still harshly criticized in Korea, but not as much as previously. More and more refugees from North Korea have fled to the South for economic prosperity and liberty.

Regarding political tolerance, another global grand wave has directly affected Korean society. Globalization, which has been a long-evolving process but really got into its stride in the 1990s, had a major impact on Korean society as well. Specifically, globalization made two specific impacts on Korean society.

First, more and more immigrants from foreign countries, especially southeast Asia and China, have come to South Korea for jobs and spouses. The fast growing economy of Korea needs foreign workers to sustain itself, and international marriage has become increasingly frequent. Thus, just as in Western democracies, immigration has gradually become a serious topic for social debate. Multiculturalism in particular has become a hot issue for Korean society to deal with, as the government needs to establish new laws and policies for immigrant workers and international marriages, and ordinary Korean citizens become more accustomed to living with immigrants. Political tolerance remains looming as an imminent problem to solve.

Second, globalization introduced cultural changes to Korean society. With its long history of Confucianism and more recent turn toward Western norms, Korea has been reluctant to accept cultural changes such as acceptance of homosexuality and abortion. Among these two issues in particular, homosexuality is more relevant for the notion of political tolerance in Korea. Even by the end of the twentieth century, homosexuals were hesitant to show their identity in public because such a 'coming out' would cause social discrimination and stigmatization. But, as Korean society, and especially the younger generation, becomes more open-minded regarding LGBT issues, some people have courageously stood up against social discrimination. Today, the LGBT community of South Korea has actually become organized, even holding a queer festival, and it is not uncommon to see openly gay expressions in public. In spite of such changes, however, the Korean public remains largely negatively disposed toward tolerance of LGBT people.

In sum, although Korean society has been relatively free from the discussion of political tolerance, mostly due to the legacy of the Cold war and Confucianism, recent changes have brought about a new phase of political tolerance in Korea. Having multiculturalism and new value-conflicting issues like LGBT rights as real challenges, Korea can no longer avoid the discussion of political tolerance regarding social minorities any more. Who are the social minorities in the context of Korea? What level of political rights are endowed to them? In what ways can political tolerance be achieved? Korean society has only just begun to discuss such fundamental questions and try to find possible solutions to maintain harmony. In the following section, using relevant survey date, recent trends in public attitudes toward social minorities will be examined.

3. Attitude toward Social Minorities in Korea: Research on Political Tolerance and Poll Trend

As political tolerance has recently grown in salience, it has attracted greater social and academic interest. For instance, several empirical studies with a focus on political tolerance in Korean society were published in 2010 and 2011 (Ka et al. 2010; Yoo et al. 2011; Yoon et al. 2011; Cho et al. 2011).

These studies, with the most frequently-used measure of political tolerance—that is, the so-called "least-liked" measures (Sullivan et al. 1982)—identified political minorities in Korea by examining people's attitudes toward a series of social groups. The measure asks people whether they would allow a member of their least-liked group to have political rights and participate in political activities. It was found that age and ideological orientation turned out to be important factors affecting political tolerance in Korea. On average, the level of political tolerance in Korea was low. The percentage of Korean respondents willing to allow members of disliked groups to participate in political activities in 2010 was below 40, much lower than western countries like the US. Given that ideology plays a significant role in choosing the most disliked group in Korea, such a finding was normatively undesirable with respect to the health of democracy in Korea. These findings suggest that, although Korean society is well equipped with democratic institutions, there is a great deal of room to improve with respect to the procedural norms of Korean democracy. The following research investigates the relationship between political tolerance and conflict and claims that Korea's low level of political tolerance makes it difficult to alleviate ideological conflicts between groups (Ka 2015; Im and Kim 2015).

This work opens the discussion on political tolerance in Korea by taking a comprehensive examination of the level of political tolerance in Korea for the first time. Meanwhile, another governmental survey includes a battery of questions on public attitudes toward socio-political minorities in Korea. The Korea Institute of Public Administration (KIPA) started a new annual survey using of face-to-face interviews in 2011 and dubbed it a fact-finding survey on social integration. The survey includes items on public attitudes toward socio-political minorities in Korea and measures respondents' willingness to embrace them using a social distance scale. Three groups of minorities are especially relevant to this review: LGBT groups, immigrant workers, and North Korean refugees. From here, I summarize recent trends in public attitudes toward members of these groups and how tolerant the Korean public are of them. A discussion on poll trends then follows.

Figure 7-1 shows the willingness of the Korean public to accept a member of three social minorities. Specifically, the questions ask whether respondents are willing to accept a member of each minority group as their neighbor, co-worker, friend, or spouse, respectively. Based on the typical social distance scale, respondents' tolerance becomes stronger as acceptance moves from neighbor to spouse. Of course, it indicates intolerance if the respondent chooses the option of "Never." From the figure, we can also see how public attitudes toward the three groups changes from 2015 (shown in the top panel) through 2018 (shown in the bottom panel).

Across the period of the survey, LGBTs are the group the Korean public seems to be the most reluctant to accept. The majority of all respondents answer that they do not want to accept them even as a

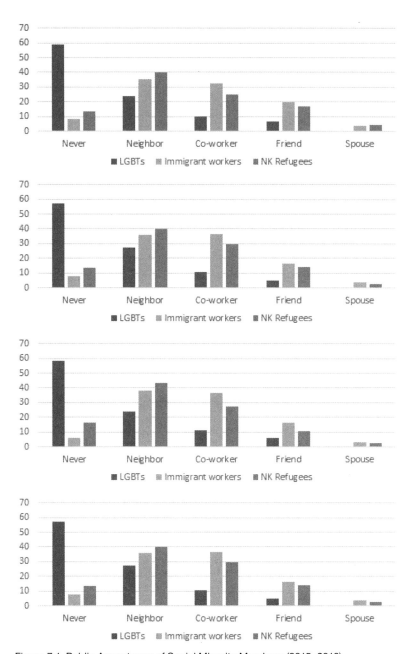

Figure 7-1. Public Acceptance of Social Minority Members (2015~2018)

neighbor. Furthermore, in all of the surveys, nobody want to marry them. The situation is not very different as we move into more recent years. Almost 60 percent of all respondents still keep their total intolerance to this group in 2018. On the other hand, the Korean public have become somewhat more tolerant toward members of the other two groups. More than 60 percent of all respondents would not care to have immigrant workers or North Korean refugees as their neighbors or co-workers. Only one out of ten respondents would even accept being friends with them. Still, the percentage does not change much across the time span of the surveys.

The next question is what types of people are becoming more tolerant of the members of social minorities in Korea? Empirical work on political tolerance in Korea find that age and ideology are important factors affecting the level of political tolerance. To see whether this is true today, I divide respondents into several groups in terms of age, gender, education, and ideology, and investigate which group are more tolerant of minority group members. The results are shown in figures 7-2, 7-3 and 7-4, for immigrant workers, members of the LGBT community, and North Korean refugees, respectively. To make the comparison simple, I only consider the level of intolerance (that is, the percent of respondents who choose "Never").

First take the case of immigrant workers shown in figure 7-2. The results indicate that there are some differences in tolerance levels between genders, education levels, and ideological orientations of respondents. Overall, male respondents are more tolerant of immigrant workers than women, although the difference is negligible. Respondents who have higher education levels show more positive attitudes toward this group than others. In addition, liberals are indeed more tolerant, and conservatives the least tolerant, to immigrant workers. The results

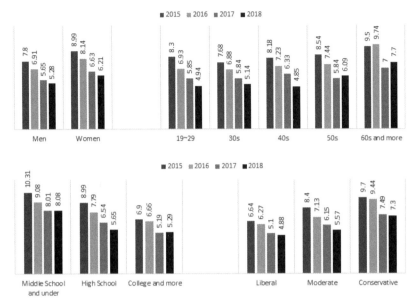

Figure 7-2. Level of Intolerance: Immigrant Workers

with respect to age are somewhat mixed. Overall, it turns out that the younger generation is more tolerant than the older generation, but respondents in their 20s are a bit less tolerant than those in their 30s. One piece of good news for immigrant workers in Korea is that the level of intolerance has decreased over time. Most groups of respondents are becoming more positive toward immigrants as we move from 2015 to 2018.

Figure 7-3 shows the same analysis for members of the LGBT community. In the previous analysis, this group engendered the highest levels of intolerance among identified social groups in Korea. Figure 7-3 confirms this again, in that most groups of respondent show high levels of intolerance toward LGBT people. Only one group, the respondents in their 20s have a level of intolerance below 50 percent. Group differences are also clear here. It seems that age, education, and ideol-

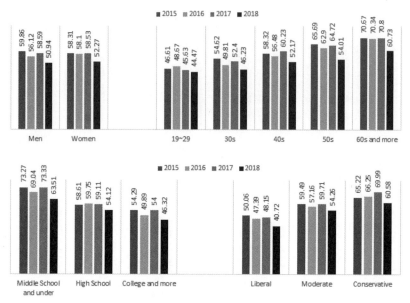

Figure 7-3. Level of Intolerance: LGBTs

ogy play a role in the level of intolerance. As people become older, they tend to have more negative attitude toward LGBT people. Education works to decrease intolerance, and respondents with a liberal ideology show more tolerance than conservatives. Given that the LGBT issue is value-conflicting and somewhat radical for Korean society, these results are understandable. However, unlike the case of immigrant workers, respondents' attitudes toward LGBT people show no signs of improvement across time. Most groups in 2018 remain where they stood in 2015. It is difficult at this moment to estimate, but the evidence seems to indicate that it will take a long time to observe greater acceptance toward LGBT people among the Korean public.

Finally we discuss the same dynamics with respect to North Korean refugees. These days, due to economic difficulties in North Korea, more and more refugees have come to the South. According to the

Ministry of Unification, it is estimated that there are more than a thousand North Korean refugees coming to the South annually. Attitudes of the Korean public toward this group are similar to those regarding immigrant workers in some ways, but to LGBT people in other ways. Overall the level of tolerance is just over that of immigrant workers, but the pattern of change resembles that of LGBT people in that it does not improve much across time.

There are two additional points to make note of here. First, attitudes toward North Korean refugees are somewhat fluctuating, dependent upon the current political situation on the Korean peninsula. Over a four-year time span, it was the year 2017 that the Korean public showed the most negative feelings toward this group, when tensions between the two Koreas was rising due to a missile crisis. After that, the level of intolerance went down to its lowest level in four years, per-

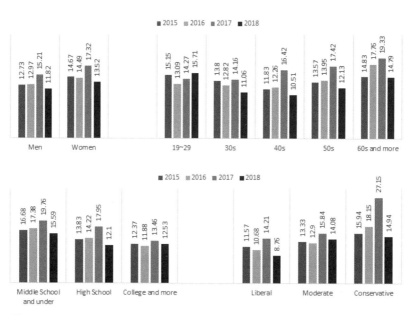

Figure 7-4. Level of Intolerance: North Korean Refugees

haps because the new Korean government tried to resume inter-Korean talks. Second, ideological orientation is a clear cue to levels of intolerance here. There is a significant difference in attitudes between liberals and conservatives. The figure clearly shows a linear relationship in attitudes as we move along a unidimensional representation of ideology from liberal to conservative. These patterns suggest that, although the level of intolerance remains low toward North Korean refugees, Korean citizens are still highly divided on this issue.

4. Polarization and Tolerance

Defined as a willingness to grant political rights to any member of society and guarantee individual freedom and liberty for them, political tolerance is one of the crucial factors for maintaining democracy. Without political tolerance, it is extremely difficult to acquire the consensus required for political decisions because members of social minorities become alienated from democratic decision-making procedures. If society keeps failing to come to a consensus, conflicts among groups become inevitable, and they may lead to the eventual collapse of the whole democracy. It is not difficult to imagine that in the era of political polarization, any conflicts tend to be more explosive than before, making it much more difficult to keep democracy functioning.

As one of the most racially and ethnically homogeneous countries, Korea has been relatively free from the discussion of political tolerance. However, recent changes (like, for instance, globalization) suggest that political tolerance will be an imminent problem for Korean society to solve. In line with these changes, this chapter examined political tolerance in the context of Korea. Specifically, this chapter examined the level of political tolerance in general, and investigated public attitudes toward three social minorities in Korea: immigrant workers, members of the LGBT community, and North Korean refugees. Analysis shows that the Korean public has lower level of political tolerance when compared to Western countries, and public attitudes toward LGBT people as a group are saliently negative even today. Because the three groups examined here are not large enough in numbers thus far, such negative attitudes have not yet led to serious trouble in Korean society yet. Nevertheless, the time is coming for Korean society to deal with political tolerance. If we are not ready to manage political tolerance properly, it will surely be difficult to maintain South Korea as a desirable place to live. It is time to take political tolerance seriously for Korean democracy.

08

Political Tolerance and Inclusion of Koreans in a Multicultural Society

Jinju Kim

Center for Future Policy Studies, Myongji University

1. Introduction: A homogeneous nation, South Korea

Koreans have long held a belief that Korea is a mono-ethnic society, buttressed by decades of exposure to public education, media, and public discourse. Ordinarily, a homogeneous nation is made up of people of the same race and language. Indeed, in Korea, more than 90% of the population is of the same race and speaks a common language. According to the results of the 2020 survey of Greenberg's diversity index, which examines the degree of diversity in a country via language, Korea ranks 165 out of 167 countries surveyed (World Population Review 2020).

The United Nations Committee on the Elimination of Racial Discrimination has steadily warned Korea of the dangers of so-called "pure bloodism". In 2007, they recommended that South Korea end the widespread use of terms like "pure blood" and "mixed blood". They also urged Korea to exclude the concept of "ethnically homogeneous" from public education. This recommendation continued in 2012. Recently, in December 2018, they recommended that South Korea, "expedite the adoption of a comprehensive law that defines and prohibits direct and indirect racial discrimination on all prohibited grounds" and "take steps to create an environment conducive to reducing the antagonism against migrants in the larger society and which facilitates the integration of migrants into society". It was recommended that South Korea review the definition of "multicultural family" in the current law, which does not include all multicultural families.

As such, the international community's recommendations for the improved treatment of migrants and multicultural families in South Korea continues. The international community views the focus on ethnic homogeneity in Korean culture as a negative because a homogeneous nation can be understood as closed, and pride in pure bloodism can be viewed as a pernicious form of nationalism. However, in terms of political culture, the concept of a homogeneous nation in South Korea also plays a positive role. During the Japanese colonial era, it became the basis of the national liberation movement, and during the Korean War and the 1997 IMF economic crisis, the perception of "we are one" encouraged people to work together to help rebuild the state. Moreover, homogeneity based on monoethnicity has expanded community consciousness, even in the formation of a unique culture within a small territory.

With the trend of globalization, various non-Korean ethnic groups have been introduced to Korean society, and exchanges between cultures have expanded, so that Korea can no longer emphasize its "mono-ethnicity" to the same degree. The political importance of being a multicultural people is gradually increasing in Korea. Based on data from the most recent election, the 2017 presidential election, the number of multicultural electors in Korea seems to be around 720,000. Since the total number of voters in the election was 42,391,464, the proportion of the Korean electorate that is non-ethnic-Korean is merely 1.6 percent. However, it must be noted that the number of multicultural electors at that time accounted for more than 70 percent of the total multicultural population in South Korea. This shows that most of the multicultural people are those who can exercise political influence despite their small numbers.

In addition, multicultural people in Korean society are also increasing the proportion of voters among their ranks and their importance in local regions, so it is no longer possible to dismiss or reject them from a political or sociological perspective. This change in Korean society could be the beginning of a multicultural society, and if there is no integration to promote democratic consciousness, it is likely to lead to great conflict and divisions between multicultural people and the many other Koreans.

Within the context of Korea becoming a multicultural society, this chapter will therefore examine the extent of social inclusion and political tolerance that Koreans hold towards the multicultural population. The aim of this paper is to suggest certain practices Korean society should pursue.

2. Social Inclusion and Political Tolerance

Tolerance and inclusion are similarly used, but inclusion incorporates a broader conceptualization than tolerance. The International Organization for Migration defines inclusion as "A process designed to allow and achieve the full participation of all in economic, social, political and cultural life of a given community or society" (2011, 87). In view of this definition, inclusion can be seen as a socially focused emphasis on equity for everyone, and this inclusiveness should be understood as a comprehensive concept that would be acceptable to anyone, whether ethnically Korean or not.

Social inclusion is a broad concept, so many scholars continue to study it from different perspectives. First, numerous studies have explored social exclusion and social inclusion together (Abrams and Hogg 2004; Cameron 2006; Dovidio et al. 2004; Hayes et al. 2008; Shotall 2004; Wlker and Wigfield 2003 etc). Social exclusion is a concept contrary to social inclusion, which, although also unclear, is generally understood as a term that refers to a multidimensional deficit across society, culture, space, politics, and economics, from poverty focused on the economic level. In this regard, the object of social exclusion was initially regarded as people in the blind spot of the social insurance system (Burchardt et al. 1999), but has since expanded to people with disabilities, the poor, the unemployed, and marginalized individuals. However, the object of social exclusion is still limited to the poor.

On the other hand, there are not many studies examining the factors influencing social inclusion in detail, but there are studies that have presented conditions for advancing toward an inclusive society. Therborn (2007) argued that social inclusion requires five steps: Visibility, Consideration, Access to Social Interaction, Rights, and Resources to Fully Participate. First, people have to show 'Visibility' to notice, realize and have their own voices heard with respect to their rights. Next, policy makers should consider the interests and needs of various groups, including minority groups. Third, people must be engaged in society's activities and social networks in daily life. Fourth, 'Rights' must be guaranteed to enable all individuals to participate and claim economic, political, social and cultural systems and institutions. However, even if these are guaranteed, the guarantee is meaningless unless the individual participates. Therefore, the final step is the 'Resources to Fully Participate', which requires the full participation of social members. If these models are applied to multicultural groups, when they have their own voice with respect to their rights, politicians listen, multicultural people's participation in all sectors of society become institutionally possible, and when they actively participate in this environment, it seems reasonable to think that it will become a society where social inclusion for multicultural people is possible.

Tolerance, on the other hand, is defined as allowing these groups the same political freedoms as any other America and the right to participate, even if they have different political opinions (Sullivan et al. 1979; Gibson and Bingham 1982; Weber 2003). In conclusion, political tolerance can be defined as the willingness to accept a group or situation that differs from oneself in terms of politics. The study of tolerance has been mainly conducted in the United States since the 1950s, and it began with intolerance studies of communists and nonconformists (Stouffer 1955). Since then, however, as society has diversified, this line of work has expanded to study the political tolerance of minority groups, such as, for example, sexual minorities.

The study of political tolerance for a certain group is an examination of how political tolerance for other groups has changed, or to compare political tolerance by country. According to the existing literature, political tolerance of communists and sexual minorities in the United States, Canada, Europe, and Asia are increasing. It is also known that countries with a long history of democracy have higher political tolerance (Pettley and Rohrschneider 2003; Marquart-Pyatt and Paxton 2007). In Korea, several studies indicate that Korea's social and political tolerance are low (Ka et al. 2010; Ka 2015; 2016; Lim and Kim 2014; Won 2014; Yoon et al. 2011). Of course, the levels of social inclusion and political tolerance differ from group to group. In the case of measuring Disliked Groups, South Koreans showed less aversion to sexual minorities, democratic unions, anti-American forces, and anti-communist forces (Ka 2016; Lim and Kim 2014).

Such studies on political tolerance have been actively performed to examine not only the tolerance itself, but also the factors influencing it. Previous studies have shown that social and economic factors such as age, education, and income (Andersen and Fetner 2008; Bobo and Licari 1989; Cote and Erickson 2009; Lee 2014; Nunn et al. 1978; Stouffer 1955), psychological factors based on social identity theory and group threat theory (Andersen and Fetner 2008; Esses et al. 2001; Lee 2014), and other factors including network-related variables based on the social theory of perception (Funk 2000; Hadler 2012; Lee 2014) and contact theory (Allport 1954; Barlow et al. 2009; Hewstone et al. 2005; Pettigrew and Tropp 2006). In particular, group threat theory, associated with social identity theory and contact theory, have been much discussed in examining the political tolerance of multicultural groups.

Individuals have the perception that they can be influenced by the culture and environment within social groups in the process of forming social identities based on social identity theory (Tajfel 1981), and that they belong to certain social groups such as religious and political identities (Abrams and Hogg 1990; Turner 1999). Therefore, social attachment to the in-group to which they belong leads to favoritism within the group and competition with out-group members (Tajfel and Turner 1986). In this competitive process, group threat theory says that people tend to reject and consider external groups as a more dramatic threat to close relationships between members of the inner group (Tajfel and Turner 1979). It was the increase of mixed-race marriage and migrant women that fostered multicultural people becoming visible in Korea, and the number of multicultural people in Korea has only increased from the time since the initial influx. Therefore, for Koreans, the multicultural groups may have developed their identities in the context of economic threats.

The increase in multicultural people may not necessarily be felt as a threat, however. According to the contact theory developed by Allport (1954), the experience of individual contact between members of a group can reduce the majority bias towards a particular minority (Pettigrew 1998; Pettigrew and Tropp 2000), and thus diminish prejudice because personal contact can reduce uncertainty and anxiety among minority groups (Islam and Hewstone 1993; Voci and Hewstone 2003; Dixon and Rosenbaum 2004; Pettigrew and Tropp 2008). In other words, familiarity can lead to tolerance (Smith and Haider-Markel 2002; Haider-Markel 2010; Lewis 2011). Therefore, as contacts with multicultural people increase, prejudice against them may disappear and political tolerance may increase.

3. The multicultural people in Korean society

After the Korean War broke out for three years from 1950, mixed-race children of US soldiers and Korean women who participated in the war began to become increasingly visible in Korea. And in the late 1980s, Korea rapidly changed into a country that accepts migrants (alongside Taiwan, Hong Kong, and Singapore; Castles et al. 2013). In the 2000s, as the status of Korea increased for women in China and Southeast Asia, international marriages increased greatly due to the increasing number of immigrant women who were brought to Korea just for the purpose of marriage. In the early 1990s, Korea's rural bachelor's market was a developed to increase international marriage brokerage

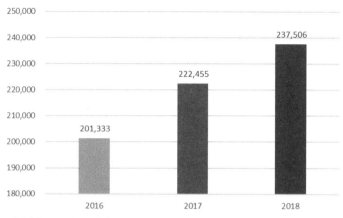

Figure 8-1. The number of children in multicultural families

rates.

This increase in international marriage between foreigners and Koreans shows that Korea's multicultural society is gradually expanding. In addition, the number of long-term foreigners who hope to establish residency and find stable work is also gradually increasing (Ministry of Justice of South Korea 2019). In addition, the number of multicultural people[1] stood at 1,008,520 as of 2018, accounting for 1.9 percent of the 51,629,512 people (the Statistics Korea 2018). Although this figure does not reach the OECD standard of 5%, which distinguishes between single and multi-ethnic countries, it is an increase compared to 2015, when 887,804(1.7%) were multicultural people among 51,069,375.

The number of children in multicultural families is also increasing. According to a survey by the Ministry of Public Administration and

---

[1] A multicultural person is one who belongs to a multicultural family, specified in the "MULTICULTURAL FAMILIES SUPPORT ACT". It refers to a naturalized Korean citizen among married immigrants and foreigners, except for those who naturally have Korean nationality from the moment of their birth. In the case of their children, they belong to the category of 'multicultural family' even if they have already acquired Korean nationality from birth.

Security, the number of children from multicultural families in Korea who are minors aged 0 to 18 is about 230,000, increasing by more than 10,000 each year. Considering that as of 2018, more than 80% of multicultural children under the age of 11 appeared, it is estimated that the number of multicultural people will gradually increase in Korean society. In addition, Korea is a low birth rate country with a birth rate of 0.98, and is the only country in the world with a birth rate of 0 people. The birth of multicultural families is also slowing down, but as of 2018, 15,324 children, or 4.6% of all 326,800 birth children in Korea, are children of multicultural families, and their demographic impacts are expected to increase in the future.

4. Korean perceptions of multicultural people

So how do Koreans view multicultural people who are still unable to speak in Korean society. As seen in previous studies (Lim and Kim 2014; Ka 2016), Koreans are relatively more tolerant of multicultural people such as migrant women and foreign workers, than other minorities. "The Study on Multicultural Acceptability in Korea", surveyed by the Ministry of Gender Equality and Family, used data from 2012, 2015 and 2018 to examine people's perceptions of multicultural families, social acceptance, and political tolerance.

As a result of asking each group whether they would like to be neighbors, LGBT was the group that was least liked, followed by Refugees and Foreign Worker / Immigrant.[2] The interesting thing in Table

---

[2] Korean society's perception of LGBT is still lower than that of other countries. In Korea, where conservative Confucianism still deeply remains, the anti-discrimination laws against sexual minorities have not been established, and the public's perception of them is also very negative. In the future, we should expand social inclusion by accepting them as a social group, but to date, despite the global trend, sexual minorities in South Korea are the worst among minority groups.

Table 8-1. Koreans' Social Inclusion for Various Minorities: 'It doesn't matter if you are a neighbor' (%)

	Other-Races	Foreign Worker/ Immigrant	LGBT	Other Religions	Refugee
2015	26.38	31.73	77.93	14.78	47.25
2018	25.89	29.51	68.97	16.74	55.69

Note: Data for 2012 were not included because there was no corresponding questions.

8-1 is that Koreans perceive Other-Race and Foreign Worker / Immigrant differently. It shows relatively low social inclusion to Foreign Worker / Immigrant than Other-Race. This seems to be because Korea's Foreign Worker / Immigrant is mainly from the Middle East and Southeast Asia. Koreans also have different perceptions by race, even within multicultural groups. According to Kim et al. (2014), foreigners' perceptions of immigration by country of origin showed positive results of 65.9% for the United States, but 52.1% and 45.7% for the Philippines and Nigeria. Koreans essentially had a closed attitude toward non-Western cultures (Kim et al. 2014). In this way, the social inclusion of Koreans also showed a difference between Other-Race and Foreign Worker / Immigrant. However, it is clear that both groups have low social inclusion, with Koreans generally not wanting to be neighbors.

Next, we examined the degree of political tolerance of Koreans to multicultural groups from a political perspective. Participation in voting is the most fundamental part of political participation, so there is a high possibility of answering morally and justly. Therefore, through the question of the right to vote, the political tolerance of Koreans to multicultural people was examined. The survey item was worded, "Even if I admit the right to vote to foreign migrants with Korean nationality, it is difficult to accept being a member of the National Assembly or a president."

Table 8-2. Koreans' Political Tolerance for multicultural group: 6 categories (%)

	Not at all 1	2	3	4	5	Very much 6
2012	2.96	11.84	17.68	22.80	29.20	15.52
2018	2.98	12.33	17.68	26.5	25.68	14.88

Note: Data for 2015 were not included because there was no corresponding question.

In both the 2012 and 2018 data, the political tolerance of Koreans was low. Looking at the scale of 1-6 points, 32.5% and 33.0% of respondents in 2012 and 2018 were positive for foreign migrants, and only 3% of respondents were the most positive. Conversely, the most negative responses were 15.52% and 14.88%, confirming that the political tolerance of Koreans to multicultural people is not high.

It is not that there were no politicians from multicultural families in Korean society. In the 2010 local election, an immigrant woman from Mongolia was elected after being nominated as a proportional representative of the GNP of the Gyeonggi Provincial Assembly. And in the 19th general election in 2012, Jasmine B. Lee, an immigrant woman from the Philippines, was elected as the 15th proportional member of the saenuriparty. However, they were also elected as proportional representatives, making it a top-down nomination. Also, despite the experience of politicians from multicultural origins in some ways, Koreans still have a problem to be solved in that their general political tolerance for multicultural people is relatively low.

If the political tolerance of Koreans is still low despite the experience of multicultural people's political activities, we would like to find out whether the individual's experience or contact with multicultural people could be related to political tolerance. According to collective threat theory, the increase in the number of multicultural people can be an economic and cultural threat to Koreans. But according to contact theory, the level of inclusion and tolerance should increase when the number of contacts increases. Using the latest data from 2018, we analyzed the correlation[3] between other variables, social inclusive variables, and political tolerant variables.

As there was a positive correlation between social inclusion and political tolerance,[4] it was expected that similar results would be obtained even if the two variables related to contact were measured separately. However, the results of the analysis showed somewhat different results from those for social inclusion or political tolerance. The number of immigrant friends and the frequency of contact are analyzed by making them interactive variables because it is necessary to include both whether they have friends and how long they have been meeting. Positive correlations were found in both social inclusion and political tolerance. This means that the more Korean immigrants have immigrant friends and the more frequently Koreans meet those immigrant friends, the higher their social inclusion and political tolerance. More in-depth analysis is needed to establish the causal relationship between frequent encounters with immigrant friends due to high social and political tolerance and frequent encounters with immigrant friends. However, it can be confirmed that the correlation coefficient alone is highly related to the variables in question and has a positive effect.

On the other hand, unlike the deep type of contact inherent in making immigrant friends and meeting them, results differed simply as a function of meeting many foreigners or immigrants in public. With

---

3 Correlation analysis can check the directionality of the relationship between two variables according to the (+) and (-) of the correlation coefficient, and the statistical significance of the correlation coefficient through the significance probability (p). In general, $p < 0.05$ is considered to have achieved statistical significance.

4 The correlation coefficient is 0.053 and the significance probability is <0.01.

Table 8-3. Correlation between contact variables and social inclusion/ political tolerance among multicultural people

	Social inclusion	Political tolerance
immigrant's friend×contact frequency	0.066***	0.111***
Frequency of seeing foreigners or migrants in public places	-0.106***	0.004

Note: ***p<0.01, **p<0.5, *p<0.1

respect to political tolerance, the statistical significance of the variable itself was not found, so it was impossible to confirm. However, in the case of social inclusion, the correlation coefficient appeared in the negative direction. This means that the more Koreans who meet foreigners and immigrants in public places, the lower their social inclusion. According to group threat theory, a particular group can be considered a threat to the majority. As a result, simply seeing a lot of them in public places increases the size of the threatening group, rather than positively affecting social inclusion by increasing contact. Furthermore, there are existing studies on the aspect of contact theory that suggests the degree of affective perception and attitudes varies depending on the degree of contact (Lee 2001; Pettigrew et al. 2006; Isike 2017). Therefore, a simple increase in contact—to the extent that it is experienced in a public place—may rather lead to a consequence that hinders social inclusiveness. Table 8-3 also shows these results.

5. Conclusion: Toward a multicultural society

The political importance of the presence of multicultural people in Korean society is increasing. In particular, in areas other than major metropolitan cities,[5] there have been active civic education campaigns

---

[5] South Korea is divided into 8 provinces (do), 1 special autonomous province (teu-

conducted for multicultural people. This tends to be taking place outside of the major cities because there are quite a lot of multicultural families in those areas on a per-capita basis, and they can no longer ignore them in terms of local autonomy. The number of multicultural people living in the capital, major metropolitan cities, and special self-governing cities in Korea accounts for an average of 1.58 percent of the population of each region. On the other hand, in case of the so-called rural areas, the average number is down to 2.2 percent and about 620,000 of 1 million multicultural people live in those local areas (Korea Land and Housing Corporation 2019). Although Korea, as a unitary state, has a centralized government, once the central administrative agency proposes a basic principle, local governments follow up to establish and implement foreign policy enforcement plans accordingly. Hence, for local governments, multicultural people are now considered vitally important, despite their small proportion.

Furthermore, the fact that multicultural people can be a major productive population also contributes to their increasing political significance, especially in case of rural areas. With the elderly population which accounts for about 15 percent of the total population, Korea has now become one of the world's fastest aging societies. More specifically, whereas the number of the population aged 65 and over in rural areas is almost up to 17.3 percent, among the multicultural, only 120,000 out of 1 million are people aged over 60. Even the difference between the number of multicultural people living in major cities and provinces is

kbyeol jachido), 1 special autonomous city (teukbyeol jachisi), 6 metropolitan cities (gwangyeoksi), and 1 special city (teukbyeolsi). The cities, major metropolitan cities, special autonomous city, and special city with administrative agencies account for only 5.8 percent of Korean territory, but about 44.4 percent of the total population lives in there.

not that large. This clearly demonstrates the fact that most of the multicultural people in Korea are relatively young productive workers, and they have become an important target for local governments as they mostly live in rural areas.

In contrast, Koreans' overall perceptions of multicultural people are still negative. Although social inclusion is higher than for other minorities, there is also ample discrimination by race. In terms of political tolerance, the reality is that it is increasingly perceived negatively by Koreans. Multicultural people are also trying to raise their political voices by, for instance, such activities as producing politicians in Korean society and the creation of the Korean League of immigrant Women Voters on April 28, 2014. However, great barriers still exist.

The Korean government provides a variety of multicultural education materials to Koreans to raise awareness and improve social inclusion. Also, for stable settlement of multicultural people, the central government and local governments support them through policies. The institutional part will be important for social integration, but above all, it is of most importance to reconsider the recognition of tolerance and inclusion of individual citizens. Only when a political culture is created with such recognition will proper social integration be possible. Social integration is an essential element in reducing the social cost of social conflict and building a good society (Sullivan et al. 1979). Based on the analyses presented here, it is necessary to seek activities that enable multicultural people and Koreans to form deep relationships, and to promote Koreans' awareness of toward multicultural people. I hope that Korea will move forward with a stable multicultural society in keeping with the broad societal changes.

Part IV

The Development of Information Technology and Political Communication

09

Political Content on YouTube

Hana Kim

Dankook University

1. Mass Communication in Political Science

From the speeches of Aristotle and Plato to political contents on social network services (SNS) and YouTube, the importance of communication through both of interpersonal and mass media means has been an important area of inquiry in political science. Beyond political science, this importance has led to the development of the interdisciplinary field of political communication, combining elements from mass communication, psychology, marketing, political science, sociology, and so on. Many definitions of political communication have been suggested and advanced, and there is no single widely accepted definition (Kaid 2004). However, as a working definition for the current chapter, the simplest is the best: political communication is the "role of communication in the political process" (Chaffee 1975, p.15).

The basic model of communication helps us understand various communicative phenomena, including YouTube, in political process.

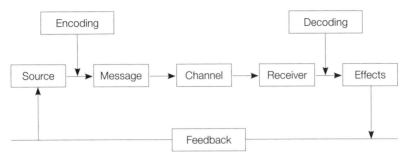

Figure 9-1. SMCR Model of Communication

Berlo (1960) expanded Shannon and Weaver's linear model of communication and created the Sender-Message-Channel-Receiver (SMCR) model of communication, which separated the model into clear parts and has been expanded upon by other scholars. This model describes the exchange of information and can be applied to all forms of political communication.

Source The creator of the message or from whom the message is sent and who encodes the message. Factors of Communication skills, Attitude, Knowledge and Social systems affect the source. In political communication, politician, political party, interest groups, etc. can all be the source.

Message The actual content or idea for the communication. The message can be sent in various forms, such as audio, speech, text, video or other media. The message is influenced by factors of Content, Elements (nonverbal aspects), Treatment, Structure, and Code. Political advertising or political speech can be considered as message in political process.

Channel The medium through which communication takes place, so that the message can be conveyed from one place to another. Mass communication always involves technical tools, such as the Internet and television. In these cases, the transmitted information is assimilated via vision and sound. Technical development triggers the booming up of various digital media channels. YouTube is one version of digital platforms as a channel.

Receiver The individual or group or the person who finally receives the message. Berlo's SMCR Model of Communication assumes the receiver's thinking pattern must be in accordance with that of the sender in order to make communication effective. Therefore, the same factors influence this component. After all, the receiver decodes the message him- or herself and gives it its own meaning. Voters or subscribers can be receivers of messages.

Effect The outcome of effective communication between a message sender and a receiver. After the message is sent, noise may occur. This noise disrupts the source message and causes the receiver to only partially receive the message or not at all. Persuading voters with political advertising to support a candidate who uses the ads can be an example of effect in political communication.

We can see the essence of political communication in the electoral process, how politicians communicate with and persuade voters using various mass media based on the SMCR Model. In order to win an election, candidates and campaign managers try to their best to disseminate political advertising and news releases on traditional media and communicate with voters on SNS directly to form voters' opinion in positive way.

2. Mass Media as Election Campaign Tools

Election is the basis of democracy, so conducting free and fair electoral competition is essential. Free and fair electoral competition means that elections take place without violating any rules and regulations, and the political parties abide by the electoral guidelines and do not misuse their powers. Without competition, the election would become meaningless. If there are no competitors, then there would be an assured of win by one side or the other. The competition of elections holds the contestants accountable.

Politicians are always looking to find the most efficient and best way to win this competition. The history of election campaigns lies with the invention of mass media. The evolutionary line of mass media started with television, then social network services (SNS), and has now become a multi-channel network (MCN). The invention of television has made tremendous changes in political election campaigns. TV news coverage, political advertising, and televised debates start grabbing voters' attention and play critical roles in winning elections. Specifically, political message based on visual leads to the era of "imagery" in politics. An image is created through the use of visual impressions that integrate into the minds of voters as they are communicated by the candidate's physical presence, media appearances, and political experience. As a candidate's image becomes more important relative to actual issue stances in determining the winners of electoral contests, political consultants are increasingly more likely to focus on establishing campaign strategy to create a positive image of a candidate.

Within the conversations surrounding SNS comes the campaign. By this time, we have all become accustomed to influencers, bloggers, page views, etc. And now we introduce Multi-channel networks (MCN). Even though the term MCN[1] has been around for a few years,

---

[1] The term was coined by former YouTube employees Jed Simmons, referring to the video platform as a network.

no one knows quite what an MCN is, what it does, or how to utilize it for either political campaign strategy or an academic field. Generally, MCN represent popular influencers, currently just YouTube stars from what we can tell, and package it for politicians and political consultants to use in their campaigns and promotions in exchange for a win of an election.

3. Up-rise of YouTube as an Information Source

The Republic of Korea is one of the world's most technologically advanced and digitally connected countries, with a high-speed internet penetration rate around 93%, and hyper-fast, low latency connection, 5G. This highly advanced technological environment provides internet users with more chances to access various digital social platforms, such as Facebook, Instagram, YouTube, podcast, etc. According to Digital News Report 2019,[2] 40% of Korean watched news clips on YouTube in a week, and this number is 14% higher than most other countries . Compared to the usage of other social platforms, the use of YouTube dramatically increased since the previous year (38% for news), at a rate ahead of most other countries. 45% of Korean YouTube users answered that they have spent more time watching YouTube in the last year. Also, Koreans watched YouTube clips at a high rate regardless of users' age. This stands in contrast to other countries in which YouTube growth is largely a phenomenon of the younger generations. In other countries, 22% of people over age 55 used YouTube, while 42% of Koreans in the same age category did so.. In terms of political ideology, people in Korea who say that they lean toward either a liberal or conservative

---

[2] Digital news report 2019 is an annual report conducted and published by Reuters Institute for the Study of Journalism. A total of 75,000 people (including 2,035 Koreans) from 38 countries responded this year.

Table 9-1. Top Social Media and Messaging

Rank	Brand	For News	For All
1	YouTube	38%(+7)	68%
2	Kakao Talk	28%(-11)	72%
3	Facebook	22%(-3)	47%
4	Instagram	8%(+1)	31%
5	Twitter	7%(-1)	19%
6	Kakao Story	7%(-5)	30%

Source: Reuter Institute Digital News Report (2019)

ideological position use YouTube more than people who say that they are neutral.

What is the motivation for using political clips on YouTube in Korea? Recent research indicates that users' motivations are of three types: information learning, networking, and entertainment seeking (Oh 2018). According to Oh's study, information learning and networking have a positive relationship with political interest, political efficacy, and political participation. The results suggest that watching political content on YouTube affects users' political socialization.

4. Effect of YouTube Political Content

How does exposure to political content on mass media affect voters in democracy and contribute to political socialization? Internet access and online exposure to information about election campaigns are significantly associated with voters' political efficacy, knowledge, participation, and trust, regardless of sociodemographic variables, party identification, partisan strength, political interest and other media exposure. Watching both hard and soft contents also positively affects various political variables. Voters exposed to hard contents, such as television debates, tend to have greater political knowledge, efficacy, and express higher rates of intention to vote than those not exposed. Similar results obtain with respect to YouTube use. Specifically, use of political content on YouTube leads to learning effects with respect to political socialization and is associated with increased political efficacy, political involvement, and political participation.

Korean politicians and political consultants have recently begun considering YouTube as an essential tool for election campaigns. The results of in-depth interview with 11 politicians and their staffs who have YouTube channels indicate that most of them see this network as a way to communicate with subscribers (voters) and promote political activities directly without using traditional media (Jang 2019). In terms of content, politicians of the ruling party produce video clips focusing on their political activities. Politicians for the opposition party criticize the government or the ruling party's political mismanagement. Interviewees suggest that consistent uploading is the most important factor to be a powerful influencer regardless of content quality or topic. Furthermore, specialized content that differentiates from other channels also does not matter. Politicians have come to understand that YouTube political content can have substantial effects on voters' support for the election.

5. Applicable Theoretical Background

A Content Creator as a Message Source

The concept of source credibility should be considered in the case of YouTube given that YouTubers create and deliver contents independently. The idea of credibility was first derived from Aristotle who argued that the speaker's reliability, ethos (credibility), must be built and established in speech. The originator or source of a persuasive communication may be a person (e.g., the president of Korea), a group (e.g., political party), a medium (e.g., TV, YouTube), and so forth. Identification of the source provides the audience with information above and beyond the arguments presented in the message. Thus, credibility has been defined as the judgments made by a message recipients concerning the believability of a communicator. A message source may be thought highly credible by one perceiver and not at all credible by another. Furthermore, the general notion of credibility has been broken down into more specific components in an investigation aimed at identifying the basic underlying dimensions of credibility.

Source credibility, for instance, is defined as the combination of a source's expertise, and trustworthiness (Hovland et al. 1953).[3] Expertise was defined as "the extent to which a communicator is perceived to be a source of valid assertions," and trustworthiness was defined as "the degree of confidence in the communicator's intent to communicate the assertions he considers most valid. Further, Hovland et al. hypothesized that an endorser associated with high trustworthiness provokes greater message acceptance than an endorser associated with moderate or low trustworthiness. However, several sets of research have found contradictory results: sometimes source credibility led to greater persuasion; sometimes source credibility led to less persuasion; and sometimes credibility did not influence persuasion at all. These confusing findings led to the introduction of the Elaboration Likelihood Model (ELM).

According to ELM (Petty & Cacioppo 1986), source credibility can affect persuasion through a variety of distinct mechanisms, de-

---

[3] In 1980, Ohanian suggests a third dimension of source credibility, namely, attractiveness, which is an affective component of source credibility. Attractiveness usually includes a source' s physical appearance and is frequently used for measuring source credibility of celebrity endorsers in commercials.

pending on message recipients' level of elaboration. When elaboration is low, source credibility operates as a cue to persuasion, such that a high-credibility-source is more persuasive than a low-credibility-source, regardless of the argument strength. In contrast, when elaboration is high, strong arguments are more influential than are weak ones, regardless of source credibility. When elaboration is moderate, a high-credibility-source is more influential than a low-credibility-source only when arguments are strong.

Likewise research on source credibility in mass communication has primarily focused on its effect on persuasion and attitude change. The source credibility of YouTubers (e.g., politicians, political parties, individual voters) can be important considerations for measuring the effectiveness of political contents on YouTube in terms of persuading voters. Therefore, if you were a political consultant establishing campaign strategies on YouTube, you should ponder how increases in source credibility could help to maximize the effects of political message exposure on YouTube.

The Hierarchy of Effects Model

The hierarchy of effects is the natural process of persuasion where one begins with the total, unaware ideas, persons, or brands, progress through a series of stages, including awareness, liking, and action, and ideally end up in a state of loyalty. This model is usually applied to the fields of marketing and advertising because the behavioral measure—a purchase—is straightforward and easy to understand. In the same way, the hierarchy of effects can explain how political contents on YouTube affect voters' cognition, attitudes, and political behavior in a process of political persuasion. The hierarchy of effects model has a variety of names (e.g., AIDA (Awareness-Interest-Desire-Action), AIDMA

Figure 9-2. Six Stages of Hierarchy Effect Model

(Awareness-Interest-Desire-Memory-Action), etc.). Whatever the name, however, the end result is the same. The following six-stage representation is more common (Lavidge & Steiner 1961).

Awareness If the normal state of voters is a state of unawareness of your candidate, public policy or the name of a political party in a political communication, then the first step of persuasion is to achieve awareness via YouTube.

Knowledge This stage involves creating political knowledge. This is where comprehension of the political content one is exposed to on YouTube and what it stands for is critically important. What are the politician's specific appeals? In what way is he or she different from other politicians or party affiliates? These are the types of questions that can be asked.

Liking If YouTube viewers look unfavorably towards the communicator, he or she has to determine why. At this stage, voters' positive attitudes toward communicators should be achieved.

Preference Voters might like the candidate (political party) but not prefer it to opponents (other political parties). In this case, the communicator must try to influence voters' preference by promoting various features of politicians or their policies.

Conviction Voters might prefer a particular candidate in an election campaign but not develop a conviction about supporting him or her. The goal of this stage is to build conviction among the voters.

Behavior The last and the most crucial stage of the political persuasion process is actual political behavior, such as voting, and political participation. Governments should must make sure that the voting experience is easy and perhaps even enjoyable for the voter.

10

ICT(Information, Communication, and Technology) and Political Communication

Shin-Il Moon

Myongji University

1. Introduction

This chapter consists of two sections and aims to give undergraduate students a general introduction to the relationship between the ICT development and political communication. The first part opens by reviewing the recent advances and trends of new media technologies (i.e., digital convergence, evolution of the web 1.0, 2.0, & 3.0, social networking services) in order to help understand ICT's influences in our everyday lives. Along the way, readers will be introduced to a variety of major concepts and specific examples used by new media scholars. The second part begins by briefly introducing the study of political communication and broadly exploring the social and interpersonal factors that affect political communication processes, focusing on the effect of smart media on political judgment and behavior. Finally, relevant studies and summarized examples (i.e., tables, figures) are utilized throughout the chapter to enhance a better understanding of how ICT interacts with political communication processes.

2. The Emergence of ICT as a driver of social change

In recent years, the development of ICT (Information, Communication, & Technologies) has changed society and our daily lives in remarkable ways. Specifically, information networks such as the Internet have provided the ability for individuals, organizations, and nations to exchange and distribute information by eliminating national boundaries and geographical separation (Dobrota, Jeremic, & Markovic 2012; Kretschmer, Klimis, & Wallis 2001; Moon, Barnett, & Lim 2010; Robertson 1992). As the flow of information, ideas, products, and people on a global scale has greatly increased, the world is becoming a more unified place. McLuhan (1966) called this phenomenon the 'global village'. Accordingly, a growing body of research in new media and technologies has demonstrated the influence of ICT as a force of social change. For example, the World Economic Forum has labeled it the 4th industrial revolution (Schwab 2016). The 4th industrial revolution can be characterized by a wide range of new technologies includ-

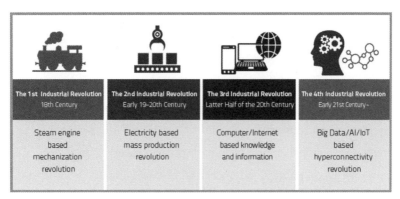

The 1st Industrial Revolution 18th Century	The 2nd Industrial Revolution Early 19-20th Century	The 3rd Industrial Revolution Latter Half of the 20th Century	The 4th Industrial Revolution Early 21st Century-
Steam engine based mechanization revolution	Electricity based mass production revolution	Computer/Internet based knowledge and information	Big Data/AI/IoT based hyperconnectivity revolution

Figure 10-1. The Technology of the Fourth Industrial Revolution
Source: https://www.samsungsdi.com/column/technology/detail/55162.html?listType=gallery

ing artificial intelligence (AI), robotics, the Internet of things (IoT), 3D printing, and self-driving cars. Figure 10-1 presents the key features of the 4th industrial revolution.

Two concepts (i.e., convergence and connection) are starting points that differentiate the 4th industrial revolution from other industrial revolutions. The term convergence can be defined as two or more things joining together or evolving into one. When applied to new media environments, convergence is used to describe the erosion of distinctions among different media. Consider a device like a smartphone. Contrary to traditional media devices such as television, radio, and print, a smart phone has various functions: Internet portals, music/video players, digital cameras, and personal organizers. This convergence among media is attributed to the conversion from analog to digital. More specifically, media content in digital form can be easily transferred and stored in diverse formats and can then be interchangeable to a variety of media devices.

Another important factor that we should consider in the current ICT environment is the evolution of the web. The Internet has become a principal place where online users communicate with content, share their own opinions, and maintain their relationships with others. With technological progress in ICT development, the Internet has rapidly evolved in the last decade. Table 10-1 summarizes the key differences between Web 1.0, Web 2.0, and Web 3.0 (for more information, see Kreps & Kimppa 2015).

As can be seen from Table 10-1 above, Web 3.0 is designed to provide more intelligent, personalized, and data-driven services for online users. Similar in spirit to the 4th industrial revolution, Web 3.0 provides users with more personalized and customized contents by using algorithmic systems and hyper-connected technologies.

Table 10-1. Comparison between Web 1.0, 2.0, and 3.0

	Web 1.0	Web 2.0	Web 3.0
Period	1990-2000	2000-2010	2010-present
Focus	Company-oriented	Community-oriented	Individually oriented
Keyword	Access	Participation	Context
Device	PC	PC & Mobile	Electronic devices
User	Human	Human	Human-Machine
Information	Static/Read-only	Dynamic/Read-Write	Portable & Personal
Feature	The hypertext web	The social web	The semantic web
Technologies	HTML	Flash/Java/XML	RDF/EDFS/OWL

Source: Prabhu 2016

3. The Proliferation of Social Networking Services(SNSs)

The term SNS has been defined in various ways by scholars. Although some scholars (e.g., Fuchs 2014; Helmond 2015) make the distinction between social networking services and social media platforms in investigating the social media phenomenon, I decided to use the broader term 'social networking services' in this chapter because the two terms seem to blur and overlap (boyd 2015; Papacharissi 2015). According to boyd and Ellison (2007), social networking sites can be defined as "web-based services that allow individuals to (1) construct a public or semi-public profile within a bounded system, (2) articulate a list of other users with whom they share a connection, and (3) review and traverse their list of connections and those made by others within system" (p. 211). With the widespread adoption of social networking sites like Facebook, Twitter, Instagram, and Youtube, there has been increased academic interest in the role of social networking sites in social interactions. For example, some research attempted to explore the effect of visual cues on initiating friendship on Facebook (Heide, D'Angelo, & Schumaker 2012; Tong, Heide, Langwell, & Walther 2008; Wang,

Moon, Kwon, Evans, & Stefanone 2010), while other studies investigated individuals' choices and their strategies to manage communication privacy (Child & Petronio 2011; Child, Pearson, & Petronio 2009; Moon, Lee, & Lim 2018).

Two recent meta-analytic studies on SNSs (Wilson, Gosling, & Grapham 2012; Zhang & Leung 2015) offer recent trends and findings of SNS research. Table 10-2 shows areas of Facebook research identified in 412 relevant articles during the period from 2005 to 2011 (Wilson et al. 2012).

Another meta-analytic study (Zhang & Leung 2015) provides a review of the scholarship on social networking services by classifying SNS studies into 4 broad themes: (1) impression management and friendship performance, (2) network and network structure, (3) bridging online and offline networks, (4) privacy. Considering the lack of existing research on the relationship between SNSs and political behaviors, the two studies consistently suggest future research is encouraged to exam-

Table 10-2. Areas of Facebook Research in the Literature Review

Area of Research	No. of articles	% of total	Associated research question
Descriptive analyses of users	97	24%	Who is using Facebook, and what are users doing while on Facebook?
Motivations for using Facebook	78	19%	Why do people use Facebook?
Identity presentation	50	12%	How are people presenting themselves on Facebook?
Role of Facebook in social interactions	112	27%	How is Facebook affecting relationships among groups and individuals?
Privacy and information disclosure	75	18%	Why are people disclosing personal information on Facebook despite potential risks?
Total	412	100%	

Source: Wilson et al. 2012

ine whether social networking sites play a key role in various political communication effects (e.g., political participation, opinion formation and change, and political campaigns and elections).

4. Political Communication & SNS

As noted earlier, the second part aims to give students an introduction to the study of political communication, and in so doing, provide some context for explaining how communication networks influence political communication processes. McNair (2003) defines political communication as a process of communication between political actors and civil society through communication channels. Similarly, McLeod, Kosicki, and McLeod (2009) emphasize the triangular relationships that exists between political actors (e.g., politicians, journalists, elites), the media (e.g.., TV, newspapers, cinema), and the general public (both foreign and domestic) by narrowing the boundaries of political communication.

Recent research on political communication suggest that social networking sites have become meaningful venues for politically relevant information, activities, and interactions (Kwon, Moon, & Stefanone 2015; Moon, Lee, & Lim 2018). Many studies have found empirical evidence that social networking sites are significantly related to a wide range of political judgments and behaviors. Table 10-3 presents the change of democracy model in accordance with the widespread use of SNS. Statistics also show that more than half of the adult population in the U.S. is exposed to political content shared by their networked friends via SNSs (Pew Research 2012). In addition, the survey reports that the majority of SNS (73%) often disagree with their friends' political posts, and furthermore, 38% of users actually make surprising discoveries about their friends' political perspectives. These results may pose some important questions: how online social network exposure effects can shape online

Table 10-3. The Widespread of Digital Network and the Change of Democracy Model

	Representative Democracy	Network Democracy
Actor	Responsive Citizens Rational Citizens Duty-Based Citizens	Participatory Citizens Emotional Citizens Engaged Citizens
Structure	Party-Centered Flows of Power Region, Ideology, Conflict	Network-Centric Power of Flows Life Issues, Competition
Institution	Representative Institutions Mediating Institutions	Participatory Institutions Connecting Institutions

Source: Yun 2012, p. 324

public discussions or how networked exposure to different political opinions can impact users' political posting behaviors.

It is important to note that interpersonal networks can potentially serve as (1) an outcome, (2) a mediator, or (3) a moderator of political communications. Individuals communicate and share their political positions with their family members, friends, and other online users through SNSs. That is, interpersonal networks via SNSs could encourage users to directly share and discuss their political positions. Political campaigns have used various media forms to reach the targeted voters. Politicians may consider powerful network leaders who influence their followers' opinions. Stated differently, opinion leaders as mediators who have a community of followers can influence the attitudes and behaviors of others. Interpersonal networks could moderate the effects of political communication. Interpersonal networks could serve to either increase or decrease political behaviors because individuals may be encouraged or constrained by the presence of others. For example, while exposure to heterogeneous political discussion networks may promote online deliberation processes, exposure to disagreements can have a negative impact on participation in political discussion.

Table 10-4. Three different perspectives on the impact of new media on public participation

	Key Arguments	Role of Internet
Optimism	Mobilization, Transformation, Participatory and Deliberative Democracy	Deterministic (Positive)
Pessimism	Reinforcement, Digital Inequality (Digital Divide), Engaging those already engaged	Deterministic (Negative)
Skepticism	Normalization, Reflection (Mirroring), Displacement, Complement, Politics as usual	Reflected and socially shaped

Source: Park & Perry, p. 193

Accordingly, some studies suggest that social networking sites as a new communication platform play an important role in promoting political participation, increasing political learning, and motivating collective behaviors (Baek 2015; Lee, Kwak, Campbell, & Ling 2014; Rheingold 2002). Other studies propose that social networking sites may lead to polarization, political cynicism, and echo chamber effects (Kim 2011; Stroud 2010; Sunstein 2007). Table 10-4 shows three different perspectives on the impact of SNS on political participation.

5. Conclusion

This chapter provides an informative context to help students understand the relationship between ICT development and political communication. By introducing major concepts, relevant studies, and specific examples, the chapter suggests that social networking sites play a key role in various political communication effects. Considering the fact that there are contradictory perspectives and mixed results regarding SNS effects on a variety of political behaviors, further study seeks to test whether social networking sites either promote or prevent individuals' political participation with more reliable measurements and analysis of longitudinal data.

11

The Issues of Machine Learning Algorithms from the Perspective of User Protection

Kitae Kim

Myongji University

1. Introduction

An algorithm is a step-by step procedures to solve a certain problem in general, or, in the field of computer science, a set of rules to effectively perform a task. In other words, an algorithm is a sort of 'recipe' that gives computers step-by step instructions to achieve a certain goal.

Algorithmic systems are increasingly being used as part of decision-making processes in both the public and private sectors, with potentially significant consequences for individuals, organizations, and societies. Most algorithmic systems are based on machine learning algorithms, which build models to predict future outcomes or perform optimization based on individual-level behavioral data. In general, machine learning is defined as the study of techniques for 'giving computers the ability to learn without being explicitly programmed' (Samuel 1959), or more contemporarily as the study of computer algorithms that '[learn] from experience (E) with respect to some task (T) and some perfor-

mance measure 'P', if 'P' improves with experience E (Mitchell 1999).'
Prior to the advent of machine learning, machines (i.e., computers)
made decisions in accordance with the strict rules. In machine learning, by contrast, machines learn from data and are able to improve
their predictions and decisions as more data[1] comes in, without the use
of strict rules specified by the programmer (see Figure 11-1).

Recently, as the amount of digitized data has increased exponen-
tially, the demand for personalized services using machine learning
has also increased rapidly. In the personalized services space, the most
widely used class of algorithms are those that underpin recommendation systems—that is, machine learning systems used to predict the
"rating" or "preference" a user would give to an item (Schafer, Konstan,
and Riedl 2001). They are primarily used in commercial applications,
across a variety of areas. Users will most likely have interfaced with
recommendation systems as playlist generators for video and music services like Netflix, YouTube and Spotify, as product recommenders for
services such as Amazon, or as content recommenders for social media

Figure 11-1. How machines learn using machine learning algorithm

---

[1] For example, individuals' behavioral data especially in personalized algorithm.

platforms such as Facebook and Twitter. These systems can operate using a single input, like music, or multiple inputs within and across platforms like news, books, and search queries. There are also popular recommendation systems for specific topics like restaurants and online dating. Recommendation systems have also been developed to explore research articles and experts, collaborators, and financial services (Hwang & Kim 2019).

Although algorithmic systems, such as recommender systems, are undoubtedly convenient tools, many researchers have recently pointed out various issues with the machine learning algorithms that could have harmful effects on users. This chapter explains some of these issues (e.g., the creation of filter bubbles in online communities, algorithmic bias and unfairness, and concerns about privacy infringement), illustrates some substantive cases where they can arise, and discusses the necessary components of an algorithmic governance system to prepare for the 4th industrial revolution era.

2. The creation of filter bubbles in online communities

The term "filter bubble," coined by Eli Pariser (2011), describes the consequences of algorithm-driven content filtering that reinforces users' exposure to the information that they already agree with, and hinders users from gaining diverse viewpoints (Pariser 2011). For example, on social network sites such as Facebook, personalization algorithms make users more likely to be exposed to contents that they have previously show some affinity for through their consumption, reactions, comments, and digital traces. This means that algorithm users might repeatedly see contents that reaffirm their existing views. Thus, users are not exposed to anything that might challenge their own thinking (Koene et al. 2017).

From the perspective of political communication, filter bubbles can result in opinion groups sharing information in common without interaction with other groups having different opinions. Exclusive interaction with members of similar opinion groups can lead to confirmation bias (Nickerson 1998), among other mechanisms of individual psychology. This can generate group polarization at the online community level (Kim 2018). In social psychology, group polarization refers to the phenomenon that the tendency is for group decision making becomes more extreme after interaction with group members than was the initial tendency of those same group members (Isenberg 1976). Obviously, content filtering by personalization algorithms can reinforce homogeneous opinion sharing, confirmation bias, and extreme opinion sharing. The problems of extreme opinion sharing and polarization, such as in the online alt-right communities or groups involved in the Brexit debate, have been widely documented in Western contexts (e.g., Marwick, & Lewis 2017; Bastos & Mercea 2019). It has been less well-documented, but remains largely the same phenomenon, in non-Western contexts.

For example, in Korea 2019, there were accusation from right-wing YouTubers that their YouTube channels were unfairly categorized as inappropriate channels for advertisements. If this process deems a YouTube channel as inappropriate for advertisements, it assigns it a so-called "Yellow Icon." In Korea If a YouTube channels has the "Yellow Icon," it is fatal from a commercial perspective because proprietors will no longer be able to collect advertisement income. Some conservative YouTubers have claimed that left wingers unjustly target them and report their channels as "Fake news" to YouTube. However, the fact is that the YouTube algorithm automatically filters out channels on which advertisers do not want their ads to appear, such as channels determined to present hate speech or politically extreme opinions, whether left or right. However, the ignorance of the YouTube algorithms' standard regarding whether to attach a "Yellow Icon" to channels generated unnecessary sustained political conflict between right and left wingers. This political dispute over "Yellow Icons" illustrates that social media platform algorithms may actually stoke group polarization in political views. Thus, explicit disclosure of how the algorithm works may be beneficial for resolving avoidable political confrontations.

3. Algorithmic bias & unfairness

It is naïve to believe that an algorithm would be objective, fair, and balanced. On the contrary, certain biases can be introduced into the operation of the algorithm, leading to unfair decisions toward some people (e.g., Mittelstadt 2017; Mittelstadt et al. 2016; Schedl et al. 2018; ProPublica 2016). One of the various sources of algorithmic unfairness is biased human judgment fed into algorithms. That is, algorithmic decision making is not free from human subjectivity. In particular, personalization algorithms that recommend or advertise a purchase to us or present us with content that we may want to see might curate contents differently for different users in ways that can be perceived as discriminatory against particular social groups (Koene et al. 2017).

For instance, Datta, Tschantz, and Datta (2015) have conducted online experiments with various simulated user profiles. They found that job-matching algorithms showed advertisements that promoted high-paid jobs to significantly fewer female users than males. As another example, Sweeny (2013) performed an experiment by entering over 2000 names into the Google search platform and observed the kinds of advertisements that were shown alongside the results of the search. Results indicated that searches for names associated with African Americans were more likely to be accompanied by advertisements including the word 'arrest' than searches for names more associated with white Americans.

Recently, many companies have begun using artificial intelligence (AI) recruiters in their employment processes (Cho 2019). From grading resumes to conducting interviews, an AI-powered recruitment system helps manage various steps of the hiring process. Some AI systems analyze candidates' facial expressions and muscle movements. Such practices can be even more concerning in South Korea where most companies require visual materials (i.e., photos) as a part of their application packages. While machine recruiters are useful for making the hiring process more time- and cost-efficient, critics argue that AI recruiters can never promise unbiased hiring. Given that AI systems depend on past recruitment data and screen documents to single out candidates that display characteristics matched to the prior recruitment profiles, it implies that companies are likely to not only employ the same kinds of workers that they have already hired, but also exclude candidates with new or unique backgrounds. Making matters worse, it is difficult to figure out how the AI recruiters operate because their underlying algorithms are proprietary trade secrets.

In summary, no algorithm is an "uncomplicated and objective instruction" (Fink 2018, p. 141). Rather, algorithms are based on "socially derived perceptions and understandings, not fixed universal, physical laws" (Eischen 2003, p. 61). In short, algorithms contain biases.

4. Concerns for privacy infringement

Personalization algorithms, such as recommendation systems, mostly operate based on large collections of personal information about individual users. One widely held criticism is that users are often unaware of the amount and types of personal information being collected about them (Solove 2004). If they were made aware, they may feel uncomfortable because of the perceived intrusion into their privacy (Datta, Tschantz, & Datta 2015; Boyd & Crawford 2012).

In the Western context, one of the most famous cases of privacy infringement could be the Cambridge Analytica scandal2 in 2018. It is reported that Cambridge Analytica, a British political consulting firm, collected Facebook users' personal data without their consent (Cadwadlladr & Harrison 2018). Facebook's platform policy allowed IT developers to access user's private data (e.g.., name, gender, political and religious views, etc.) only for academic purposes or for improving the user experience.

As another example, Facebook launched a platform called Open Graph to third-party apps in 2010. The platform allowed developers to access certain types of personal data on the social network. These data include users' private information including name, gender, political and religious views, as well as their private messages. In 2013, Aleksandr Kogan and his company, Global Science Research, created an app called 'thisisyourdigitallife'. The app invited users to answer a series of questions in return for receiving a psychological profile. In 2015, Kogan, and his company allegedly illegally sold these personal data to Cambridge Analytica, a British political consulting firm. The firm used methods based on psychometric profiling. Data about individuals were collected from a variety of sources. Personality profiles of them were created. Once profiled, individuals could be targeted by personalized advertisements. Cambridge Analytica worked in support of a number of famous campaigns, including Donald Trump's US presidential campaign and the Leave.EU campaign in the UK European Union referendum in 2016.

In response to this scandal, Facebook recently released "Off-Facebook Tracker," a tool newly embedded in Facebook's user privacy setting to allow users to see websites, apps, and even brick-and-mortar stores Facebook tracks to gather users' log data, and let them turn off that tracking (Holmes 2020).

Recently, VRT NWS, a Belgian public broadcasting company, accused Google Home (Google's AI speaker) of recording and transcribing private conversations of married couples in bedrooms and business talks over trade secrets (Verge 2017). Analogously, there are two mainstream AI speakers in Korea that were developed and are operated by the leading South Korean digital companies (i.e., Naver's Clova and Kakao's Kakao Mini, see Figure 11-2). They were similarly accused of collecting users' audio data and transcribing them into written files (Yeo 2019). While the companies explained that the transcriptions were intended to improve their system performance, what the AI speakers overheard included intimate aspects of personal lives. Unlike Alexa, Amazon's AI speaker, Clova and Kakao Mini have no privacy protection setting that can make it easy for users to selectively delete records of their digital conversations. The incident prompted privacy concerns among users of the AI speakers in South Korea, pointing to the pos-

Figure 11-2. Naver's Clover (Left) and Kakao's Kakao Mini (Right)

sibility of sensitive information being recorded, shared, and even used against the users of the AI speakers.

5. Conclusion: Toward accountable machine leaning algorithms

These concerns (i.e., group polarization, privacy concerns, potential bias or discrimination) can be exacerbated by the opaque nature of personalization algorithms and the lack of a regulatory framework (Pasquale 2015). In general, individuals do not know what the personalization is based on (e.g., search/purchase history and locations), how or for what purpose personal information is exploited by the algorithms, what kind of biases penetrate the machine learning process, and the possible discrimination against individual users that could result. Unfortunately, most social media platforms do not specify rules or procedures that account for the results presented to users of those platforms. Furthermore, the computational processes underlying machine learning are inherently complex, and to an extent that makes their procedures unfathomable by human cognitive capacity. As the saying goes, algorithms are black boxes: you put something in, you get something out, but whatever happens inside is a mystery (Montgomery 2019).

The key to gaining public trust in new algorithms is to assure their accountability and transparency. However, discussion around the issues of accountability and transparency in algorithms is still in its early stage. As a first step to lay the groundwork to establish specific rules and standards toward algorithm transparency, the General Data Protection Regulation (GDPR) established by the European Union (EU) has been in effect since May of 2018. Replacing the previous Data Protection Directive, GDPR is an attempt to impose a legal obligation of explanation (i.e., a 'right to explanation') regarding automated decision making. It is important to note that GDPR places emphasis more on procedural fairness than consequential fairness. More specifically, GDRP does not aim to detect bias in data used for algorithms or discriminative elements in algorithm design. Rather, the goal of GDPR is to ensure transparency in data processing, providing enough information to users to preempt the harmful effects of a lack of respect for the interests and rights of the users. In other words, the 'right to explanation' is meant to be a mechanism of transparency for users in data acquisition and utilization. It is for 'profiling' rather than providing users with the explanations about how and for what purpose the machine learning procedure works.

Despite the endeavor toward accountable algorithms such as GDPR, making machine learning algorithms embedded in AI services accountable and transparent is still fraught with complexity because corporations oftentimes limit information when they feel they are exposing too many details (trade secrets) of their proprietary systems, which may undermine their competitive advantages and hurt their reputations and ability to do business (Diakopoulos 2015). Trade secret is a core impediment to understanding automated authority like algorithms since it, by definition, seeks to hide information for competitive advantage (Pasquale 2011). Moreover, corporations are unlikely to be transparent about their systems if that information hurts their reputation or ability to do business. Thus, more flexible and functional approaches are necessary, taking into consideration that it is hard to explain how algorithms work in most AI, and most users are incapable of understanding the complex mathematical system. Most of all, it should be clear what the concrete objective to achieve through algorithmic transparency is, and whether the objective is to relieve users of anxiety, to choose whether to use a system or not, or to allow users to be able to respond to the intrusions to users' rights caused by algorithm.

Part V

Party Politics and
Public Deliberation

12

Party Politics and Civic Engagement in South Korea

Kyungmee Park

Jeonbuk National University

1. Introduction

In recent years, Korean civil society has extensively expressed its political voice in the streets. Active political engagement has occurred both as part of and independently from the candlelight protests for the presidential impeachment of 2016. Citizens with an interest in diverse issues light their candles in the Kwangwhamun square, a symbolic space for Korean civil protests. The level of this kind of non-institutional engagement may be high, while the level of institutional engagement through parties has been relatively passive. Parties have not been an approachable path toward political engagement for many Korean citizens.

Most recent democracies have not experienced party formation through the voluntary engagement of citizens, having been pre-modern societies that did not develop democratic institutions or systems of party politics. With respect to South Korea in particular, the two World Wars and Japanese colonial rule suppressed the developments of civil society and politics, which in turn led to the underdevelopment of parties. The end of World War II set in motion the process of democratization for many late democracies, with many achieving democratic status between the 1970s and the 1980s.

South Korea, one of the Third Wave democracies, became a full democracy in 1987 after a series of drastic political changes. Following the end of World War II, military rule by United States and the Soviet Union began in South Korea and North Korea, respectively. In South Korea, three years of military rule by the United States interrupted the normalization of politics and the development of governing institutions. The first general election was held in 1948, but June of 1950 saw the onset of the Korean War, which again brought interruption of political development. The second assembly, held in May of 1950 could be opened in Busan, but not in Seoul. Civil society could hardly engage in politics during the Korean War. Moreover, two military coups in 1961 and 1979 suppressed the growth of civil society and parties, thereby maintaining the status of the incumbent rulers as authoritarian. It was not until the Democratization Movement of 1987 that civic engagement and party politics could be active.

In the stream of drastic political changes in South Korea, citizens still had not forged a close relationship with parties. The frequent splits and mergers of parties may imply instability and a lack of institutionalization of Korean politics, which is an indirect signal that the parties have not been embedded in civil society. Further, citizens have faced parties with new names every election because, as a result of party splits, mergers, and simple name changes decided by party leaders and members of the National Assembly, not by citizens. Faced with political crises, members of the National Assembly often defects from their former parties, frequently leaving behind the promises to their constituents that got them elected. Citizens simply vote for the candidates who the parties nominate.

However, this state of affairs is not necessarily a sign of political instability because it has been part of a clear pattern. Korean citizens often predict party splits and mergers before and after elections, and incorporate these predictions into their strategic calculations. Korean citizens know that certain groups will have an interest in, say, which parties may split or merge, and patterns related to these expectations manifest themselves clearly over time. If such patterns are indeed easily predictable, Korean citizens may in fact have the institutional channels to express their political voices.

The two primary questions that motivate this chapter are as follows. How do parties and citizens in South Korea relate to one another? How can Korean citizens participate in political parties? With these questions in mind, I first analyze the relationship between parties and citizens historically. Second, I look at splits and mergers of the Korean political parties since the 1987 democratization. Third, I discuss membership of the Korean parties focusing on how citizens engage in and with parties.

2. The Growth of Parties and Civil Society

Modern party politics began after the end of World War II. There were not the official organizations and rank-and-files of parties. Although various political groups had different ideologies and strategic tactics, they had been acting passionately for political independence from Japanese colonial domination without systemic maintenance as a party organization.

The American military regime, whose domination began after August 15, 1945, took many measures to control political groups. As part of those measures, the military regime introduced a registration system for parties (i.e., the 55th command of military government office) in February of 1946. On this command, every group that wanted to act politically was required to register in the military government office. The military regime had the initiative to determine which groups could operate in Korean politics, and those who failed to register could be punished.

There is no reliable record of exactly how many groups were approved, but the consensus number is approximately 100. According to the official record of the military government office, the total number was 98, which included 49 right wing groups, 32 left wing groups, and 17 moderate groups (HUSAFIK, 68-72). Alternatively, Grant E. Meade, an intelligence officer in the military government office, recorded the existence of 107 groups in 1946 (Meade 1993, 206). Further, according to at least one newspaper, 90 groups were registered at the public opinion department of the military government office (Kyung-hyang-sinmun 1947/06/11).

After the enforcement of this registration system for parties, a diverse set of political groups were entitled to operate officially as political parties, and could run candidates for election to the interim legislative assembly in October 1946 (Kang 2015; Park 2010b). Party politics thus began in South Korea. However, not all citizens had the right to vote. Voting rights were only given to the head of a household. Furthermore, among the 98 eventual seat holders in the legislative assembly, only 50 were selected in elections, while 48 were appointed by the military government office. Thus, this initial election, though a step toward democracy, was not an example of direct voting or universal suffrage. In this vein, the interim legislation could not fully represent the Korean citizenry.

In May of 1948, the first election for the National Assembly was held under the electoral law that the interim legislative assembly passed. 49 parties participated and only 16 parties earned seats in the first national assembly. No party received more than the half of the 198 seats. The party that earned the plurality of votes earned only 53 seats (26.5%). 102 members (51.5%) were not affiliated with parties (i.e., the independent members). Parties were merged continuously in the first National Assembly. 16 parties were transformed into 3 parties by frequent mergers in May of 1950 when the first National Assembly was closed. Following this process three parties held 169 seats (84.5%) in total (Park 2010b).

The severe experiences of the Korean War had reinforced the ideological confrontation between pro-liberalism and pro-communism. The ideological discord thus not only occurred on the battlefield, but in the legislature as well. Some left-wing politicians attempted to cross the 38th parallel into North Korea when the political positions of the left wing became too narrow. Even parties could not occupy far-left ground openly because of the landscape of anti-communism resulting from the experience of the Korean War.

In the midst of all this, Korean civil society had gradually grown up enough to express its voice against the authoritarian government. Citizens did not tolerate the injustices and corruption of the first president, Lee Syengman, and his close associates in government. This was the April 19, Democratic Movement of 1960. A civil movement led by intellectuals and students spread rapidly throughout the country, eventually compelling the first president to leave office. The second republic began in 1960, but the political and social confusion was not easily settled. This political instability led to a military coup in May 1961 by General Park Junghee.

The rule of military government halted the growth of civil society. Political activity was suspended completely just after the military coup. In 1963, central power was transferred to civil government officially, but civil government was still in hands of the military who had initiated the coup. They controlled the National Assembly and its members. Citizens participated in limited elections, but the parties could not substantively represent them. Moreover, the military force formed the ruling party and controlled any parties working in government. After the death of President Park by assassination in 1979, another military coup retarded the growth of civil society again. The new military government suppressed the activities of civil society and parties. Civil society could not develop spontaneously due to controls and punishments during the 26 years of the two military governments.

It was not until 1987 Democratic Movement that civil society groups and parties could breathe freely and comfortably. A Nationwide movement of citizens demanded democratization, including the introduction of a direct presidential election system. Kwangwhamun square was filled with people eager for democratization. The military government could not help but revise the constitution to allow for direct presidential election by citizens in 1987. As a consequence, the military government left office, and the political landscape was ripe for change.

3. The Relationships between Parties and Civil Society after 1987 Democratization

We can shine a spotlight on the relationship between parties and civil society according to the following two perspectives, which are closely related in the context of Korean politics. One is the trend of party splits and mergers, and the other is the rank-and-file system of membership of in parties. The former is a feature that is unique to Korean politics. Parties in more mature democracies only rarely split and merge. Among the 208 parties that were established or newly formed between 1941 and 1980, sixty-one percent persisted (Janda 1980, 162), meaning that their rank-and-file have not changed much.

Though the emergence of new parties that espouse, for example, extreme-right or populist ideologies has occurred fairly frequently in recent years, the established parties in mature democracies have been comparatively stable. The established parties can sustain their organizational stability through citizens' consistent voting for the party with which they most identify. In particular, citizen engagement in parties has been important because membership fees and donations offer ample finances for sustaining organizations (Karp and Banducci 2007, 218).

In the sections that follow, I explore, first, trends in party splits and mergers, which illustrate the characteristics of parties; and, second, party membership, which illustrates the relationship between parties and civil society directly.

Party Splits and Mergers

Party splits and mergers have been a consistent pattern in Korean party politics. Most Korean parties have changed their organizations recently. By merging with other parties, some parties were able to persist longer than they otherwise would have. Party mergers are indeed a political strategy to expand organizational finances for enlargement. In contrast to party mergers, party splits certainly do not increase overall resources, but may raise the probability of winning for certain candidates by disassociation with a larger organization. This is all to say that party mergers and splits cannot be considered only as symptoms of political crises. They are often just a way to work within the rules of a political system to increase the chances of candidates gaining office.

Figure 12-1 shows the rough trend in organizational changes since 1945. Only several main parties are included, and splits and mergers of other parties are mostly omitted for simplification. 54 parties are enrolled in the Central Election Management Committee, but only 8 parties have seats in the 20th National Assembly in March of 2020. Parties on the left side of the figure might be considered the parties on the right side of the ideological spectrum, while those on the right side could be positioned as those on the left. Among the 5 parties in the lowest part of Figure 12-1, the United Future Party is in most conservative position while the Justice Party takes the most progressive stance.

Korean political parties can largely be divided along two axes. Two parties can generally be considered the main parties: the United Future Party and the Democratic Party of Korea. Through several name changes, splits, and mergers, these two parties have competed in every election since 1987. From 1987 to 1997, the United Future Party was the governing party (with several different party names). The Democratic Party of Korea won electoral victories in two presidential elections from 1998 to 2007. This series of elections was the first in which a ruling party and an opposition party each won and lost power through elections, with peaceful transitions between the losers and winners. The ruling party was changed to the United Future Party in 2007. However, in May of 2017 after the impeachment of president Park Geun-hye, the Democratic Party of Korea recovered its position as ruling party.

Compared with the continuity of the two major parties, other parties have experienced diverse changes. In particular, parties of the ideological left seldom had sustained themselves for very long. The Korean Independence Party, the Progressive Party, and the subsequent parties with progressive ideologies experienced formations and dissolutions repeatedly. It was not until the Economic Recession in 1997 that the progressive parties could participate in elections actively. They gained their first seats in the National Assemblies in the 2004 national election. The current number of seats in the Justice Party is just 6, but its influence in the 20th National Assembly cannot be understated. Regardless of the nominal party in power, the ideological landscape of the National As-

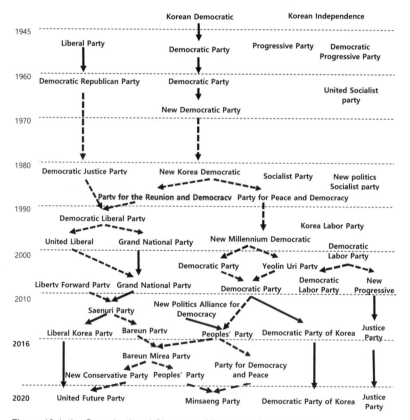

Figure 12-1. the Organizational Changes of Parties in South Korea

Note: In this figure, the dotted lines with arrows is the case of party splits or mergers, and the solid line with arrow is the case for party that sustain their organizations without party organizational changes.

Source: Revised Figure 3-1 in Park 2006, p. 46.

sembly has leaned to the right overall.

One way to think about this is to conclude that the ideological differences between parties are not actually that big. Indeed, a persistent feature of Korean democratic politics is that citizens are more likely to vote on the basis of which geographic region a candidate comes from than their ideological stances (Kim 1995; Moon 2017). This "regionalism," as it is known, dominates Korean elections, and both the United Future Party and Democratic Party of Korea are characterized by regional voting as of March of 2020.

For parties, electoral strategies tend to consider the regional distribution of the voters. Regional strongholds are often considered first, even before ideological factors and campaign promises. If party A party holds the A region with strong supports, the other parties will receive less votes in the A region. In this case, party A could have won the electoral victories in the A region. Thus, we call it as a regional party. Parties are distinguished depending on which regions presidential candidates and party leaders come from (i.e hometown).

Very recently, patterns in voting behavior have been changed little by little (Hur 2019; Lee 2017; Moon 2016). The powerful influence of the two main regional parties have remained in the 20th National Assembly as of March of 2020, while newly emergent parties have entered into the niche electoral market. Besides regional issues, other issues such as gender, generation, and social welfare were raised in the political realm. These issues are likely to attract citizens who are tired of the regional competition, and any successes that they have can make the established space changed. Most of the new issues have already have been absorbed into the campaign promises of regional parties, but the newly emerged parties are the alternatives for voters who are eager for political changes.

In April of 2020, the 21st general election was held. Amid fierce struggles inside each party, several parties already split or merged for electoral victories. The United Future Party merged with the New Conservative Party, which was split from the Bareun Mirae Party. Other members of the Bareun Mirae Party established the People's Party, and then merged with the Party of Democracy and Peace. Other parties, including the Justice Party, struggled to obtain more seats, considering which electoral position was most advantageous. However, political discussions with party members had not been very substantive because party leaders had a tendency to focus on attracting the citizens who had not decided which party they voted for yet.

Party Membership

Party membership is not critical issue because the electoral campaign is likely to focus on the citizens, not party members. Due to the weak ties with members, parties can easily decide to split and merge while only considering political deals between party leaders. Even though citizens join parties as rank-and-file members, their influence over these types of strategic decisions of leaders are very marginal. The rank-and-file typically have little influence over splits and mergers, defection of members in the National Assembly, and party leaders' arbitrary candidate nominations. In effect, all official and unofficial affairs of the parties are carried out only with respect to the authority of party leaders.

There are several reasons why party memberships are weak. For one thing, there are institutional factors such as the Political Party Law. Under a few of the provisions of this law, parties meeting some conditions can receive national subsidies four times a year. To qualify for subsidies, the conditions a party has to meet are two: having more than one seat in the National Assembly, or more than two percent voting rates in the general election. The more seats or the higher voting rates parties get, the more national subsides they receive. Without considerable sums of membership fees, a party can sustain their organizations with national subsidies.

It is reasonable to assume that this clause has an effect on the decisions of political parties about splitting or merging with other parties. The Political Party Law specifies that the parties can preserve their

Table 12-1. the Changes in Party Members (Units: persons, %)

Year	Elections	Numbers of Voters	The United Future Party and its Families		The Democratic Party of Korea and its Families	
			Numbers	Ratios	Numbers	Ratios
1988	General	26,198,205	2,804,476	10.7	458,533	1.8
1992	General/Presidential	29,003,828	4,960,665	17.1	935,419	3.2
1995	Local	31,048,566	3,518,323	11.3	202,982	0.7
1996	General	31,488,294	3,760,948	11.9	541,531	1.7
1997	Presidential	32,290,416	4,175,361	12.9	845,276	2.6
1998	Local	32,537,815	3,165,873	9.7	1,058,868	3.3
2000	General	33,482,387	2,676,324	8.0	1,736,138	5.2
2002	Presidential	34,991,529	2,778,185	7.9	1,889,337	5.4
2004	General	35,596,497	1,086,329	3.1	276,269	0.8
2006	Local	37,064,282	1,108,115	3.0	1,092,126	2.9
2007	Presidential	37,653,518	1,650,011	4.4	1,218,297	3.2
2008	General	37,796,035	1,794,091	4.7	1,643,021	4.3
2010	Local	38,851,159	2,090,976	5.4	1,918,474	4.9
2012	General	37,796,035	2,474,036	6.5	2,132,510	5.6
2014	Local	41,296,228	2,708,085	6.6	2,430,111	5.9
2016	General	42,100,398	2,991,365	7.1	2,705,938	6.4
2017	Presidential	42,479,710	3,227,708	7.6	3,568,111	8.4
2018	Local	42,907,715	3,340,979	7.8	3,579,111	8.3

Source: Produced from the database of the Central Election Management Committee of Korea.

finances and other properties when party mergers occur. Despite the changes in party names and organizations, party mergers can provide the parties with opportunities to maintain their assets as they are. These clauses can motivate parties to choose mergers rather than dissolutions when they are faced with political crises. This is because a party is likely to have less interest in memberships than party finances and properties.

Another reason for weak party membership comes from the characteristics of real politics. Korean citizens are not very active participants in parties as members. Table 12-1 shows party member ratios for the two main parties during the years of the 16 elections since the 1987 democratization. South Korea has three kinds of elections: presidential, general, and local. The electoral cycles are different for each election because of the differing terms for presidents (five years), members of assemblies (four years), and officials elected in local elections (four years).

Before the middle of 2000s, the membership ratios of the United Futures Party and its families had been higher than those of the Democratic Party of Korea. The United Futures Party and its families had possessed the bulk of material and immaterial assets because they took over all properties of the previous ruling party of the military government (see Park 2010a). The military government had accumulated its properties through administrative power and networks. At this time, the family parties of the United Future Party took over all assets at the same time it was first including rank-and-file membership. Accordingly, they hold a considerable number of memberships regardless of their efforts.

However, the trend has changed since the mid-2000s. The ratios of members have dropped below five percent, likely a result of the party reforms that made 'paper members' impossible. From 2004, most parties introduced new candidate nomination systems in which members and citizens can participate directly (see Mosler 2008). If a person wants to have the right to vote for an electoral candidate, membership fees should be paid. The rank-and-file are not considered members without payment.

The fact is not lost that the numbers of members can be overestimated considerably. In a fierce nomination contest, electoral candidates make efforts to increase the numbers of members who support them. The purported presence of many supporters may be a winning strategy. Apart from the advantages for individual candidates, the increase in members can be a useful strategy for a party. Active mobilization and its success means that numbers of supporters increase and the winning probability is raised.

However, the rights of party members are limited in some electoral districts in terms of candidate nomination. Members can vote for candidate nomination contests only in electoral districts where party leaders decide nomination contests (Jeon 2005; Park and Jeon 2019). Moreover, party leaders use this to nominate candidates in electoral districts with higher winning probabilities. The more important issue is that the right to vote in candidate selection is not restricted to members. Almost all parties conduct opinion surveys of citizens regardless of whether they are party members or not. As a matter of fact, all citizens have the right to engage in candidate nomination contests of parties. Since the right to vote in nomination contests cannot be used as an incentive to party members, this becomes just another structural reason that party leaders do not have to take the opinions of party members seriously.

4. Conclusion

South Korea has experienced rapid political change in the face of frequent interruption of the spontaneous and natural growth of parties and civil society. Before the 1987 democratization, the relationship between parties and civil society was already not close due to frequent suspensions. The authoritarian and military governments did not allow citizens to enjoy free choice and engagement with political parties while the opposition groups were being suppressed via undemocratic measures. Citizens hardly could have had the opportunity to become involved in parties spontaneously.

Before the 1987 democratization, the underdevelopment of parties came from the registration system of parties begun in 1945, and party formations by the ruling forces. Parties that emerged from the ground up usually were pushed out to the margins of the political realm. Party activities and civic engagement were possible only after official permission by the political authorities. This may be the reason that only two main parties have sustained for so long. The separate evolution of parties and civil society could have been fused at the time of the 1987 democratization. Citizen demand for democratization resonated with the opposition parties, and brought nationwide diffusion of the democratic movement.

However, we cannot yet say that parties and civil society are closely linked. Parties frequently emerge, split, and merge by resolutions from leadership. Their decisions are likely to be affected only by political needs to survive. For a member in the National Assembly, electoral victories tend to be given priority over party members and people in their electoral districts. Parties change every election, but this change is often superficial rather than a sign of de-alignment.

Citizens seem to have tired of institutional politics, including party politics. The share of independent voters among citizens has been increasing. These voters are mostly younger, have higher levels of education, and relatively weak ideological attachments (Yoon et al. 2016;

Park and Song 2012). Citizens have more opportunities to elect party candidates than ever before, but seem to prefer individual participation to party engagement as members. A vivid illustration is of this is the sight of Kwangwhamun square filled with protestors expressing their voices directly. Citizens, in other words, do not cling to institutional engagement only.

Despite the weak foundations of party politics, we can say that Korean politics has been relatively stable. Two presidential impeachments did not shake the democratic foundation, and all institutional processes maintained their routines. Most changes in party politics seem to be predictable, in which there are no fundamental changes at all. However, we should think over how to embrace the citizens' political passions and messages in order to further democracy in the future.

13

Public Deliberation in South Korea

Soo Hyun Jung

Myongji University

1. Introduction

Over the decades, many political scientists have put their faith in the ability of public deliberation to benefit society and improve modern democracies. It has been argued that public deliberation can lead to greater tolerance (Mutz 2005; Mendelberg 2002). It has also been argued that, by engaging in public deliberation, citizens may become more knowledgeable about the various policy options and possibly change their opinions about them to achieve benefits in the public interest, even if they perhaps differ from private interests. Various types of deliberative forums have been suggested and implemented in Western democracies, such as citizens' juries, consensus conferences, deliberative polling, citizens' assemblies, and so on.

In South Korea, some civil groups and local governments have also adopted deliberative policy-making experiments to make decisions about policies that touch on issues of social conflict or complex technological knowledge. But it was only recently that most Koreans became aware of and attentive to public deliberation. In 2007, the Korean government employed a deliberative poll, conducted from July 24 to October 20, 2017, to determine whether to resume the construction of Shin-Gory Nuclear Reactors No. 5 & 6, which had been suspended to comply with President Moon Jae-in's campaign pledge. Public deliberation was adopted because President Moon believed that the process could establish a social consensus on that issue (The Public Deliberation Committee 2017, 16-17).

This research aims to review the background, processes, and outcomes of several deliberative forums that were conducted in South Korea. In what follows, I first introduce public deliberation and its main concepts by reviewing the literature on deliberative democracy. Next, I examine consensus conferences, citizens' juries, and deliberative polls, which are implemented in South Korea, and compare them to other countries' cases.

2. The Effects of Public Deliberation

Over the decades, deliberative democracy has drawn many political scientists' attention. Citizen participation is central to deliberative democracy; however, it differs from participatory democracy in that it is far more concerned with the quality of political talks and the diversity of views represented than the mere amount of political conversation and participation (Mutz 2006). Many scholars are suspicious of the competence and ability of people to make reasonable decisions in the policy process. The public has inadequate levels of political information and its thinking about politics is often incoherent (Mendelberg 2002, 173).

Those who emphasize the positive role of public deliberation argue that deliberation can remedy these deficits (Fishkin 1995; Habermas 1996). Deliberation is thoughtful examination of political issues, listening to others' opinions on them, and coming to a public judgment on what represents the common good with a broadened sense of peoples' interests through reasoned argumentation (Roberts 2004; Deli Carpini et al. 2004).

According to Habermas, deliberation facilitates a clear and consistent set of political ideas by requiring that people provide reasons for their interests that other can accept (Habermas 1996). Also, the public reasoning process in public deliberation is likely to promote the common good, while participatory democracy emphasizes direct rule by citizens (Coppedge et al. 2011, 253).

This argument is based on two key claims: (1) participants who engage in public deliberation can actually learn new information about policy issues, and (2) those who already have well-informed opinions and understand the opinions of others through debate and discussion will be in at least some cases willing to revise their preferences and change their policy attitudes in light of new information and claims made by other participants (Chambers 2003, 309).

3. Deliberative Forums in South Korea

Several deliberative forums have been suggested and implemented to enhance deliberation and facilitate discussion of policy issues and subsequent decisions on them. Though these forums differ in terms of length, sponsors, organizers, and selection and number of participants, they share the following features: participants are chosen by almost random selection or specialists ensuring that individuals with certain characteristics are included; deliberation is guided by facilitators, and participants receive specially prepared and balanced information from experts; the participants, at the end of the deliberative forum, come to a conclusion about a discussed issue by majority rule and submit a recommendation on it (Pateman 2012, 8).

In this section, I will describe 1) consensus conferences, 2) citizens' juries, and 3) deliberative polls. I focus on these types of deliberative forums as they are the most popular and widely implemented versions of deliberative democracy implemented in many countries, including South Korea.

Consensus Conferences

In 1987, consensus conferences were launched in Denmark to deal with complex technological issues such as gene technology, food irradiation, and electronic surveillance. The process included ordinary citizens selected randomly, or according to some representative criteria, into informed debates with scientists and experts (Einsiedel and Eastlick 2000; Seifert 2006). It was designed to break expert dominance and foster public debate in the field of science and technology policy. The policy recommendation made by the lay panel was submitted to the government, though it was not legally binding. The conference was deemed a success and was held more than 20 times until 2003.[1] Since then, this Danish deliberative model has been carried out in many industrial nations such as Austria, Australia, Canada, France, the Netherlands, the United Kingdom and the United States, and it is usually used to discuss genetic engineering and biotechnology issues (Seifert 2006; Dryzek and Tucker 2008; Einsiedel et al. 2001).

In South Korea, the Korean National Commission for UNESCO (KNCU) hosted the first consensus conference in 1998 with the title

---

[1] http://www.loka.org/TrackingConsensus.html (accessed March 2020).

of "The Safety of Genetically Modified Foods and Bioethics," in co-operation with the People's Solidarity for Participatory Democracy, attempting not only to monitor science and technology policy, but also to encourage ordinary citizens to participate in the policy-making process. The citizen panel was composed of fifteen participants who were selected by targeting a specific distribution of age, sex, and job type among the applicants who learned about the conference through newspapers, mass media, and PC communications. In the preliminary meetings that were held in September and October, the participants were educated about GM foods by experts, and the main conference took place from November 14 to November 16 in Seoul. On the first two days, the fourteen experts made presentations responding to the questions asked by the citizen panel, followed by additional questions and answers. On the final day, the citizen panel announced the final report at the press conference, warning about the potential health risks of GM foods, and suggesting the government require labeling of GM foods in the marketplace. The final report was mailed to members of the National Assembly, public officials, research institutions, and civil groups (Lee 2008, 300 - 302). Since then, as seen in Table 13-1, several consensus conferences hosted by KNCU, Citizen Science Center of People's Solidarity for Participatory Democracy (PSPD), and Ewha Institute for Biomedical Law and Ethics were held in 1999, 2004, and 2007, discussing reproductive technology, nuclear energy policy, and xenotransplantation, and producing final reports on these topics.

In terms of the characteristics of the hosts, the consensus conferences in South Korea were different from their Danish predecessors. In Denmark, the Danish Board of Technology, which is operated as a parliamentary technology assessment organization, hosted the conferences, and their final reports had significant effects on the policy-making pro-

Table 13-1. Consensus Conferences in South Korea

Year	Host	Topic
1998	KNCU	genetically modified foods
1999	KNCU	reproductive technology
2004	Citizen Science Center	electricity policy
2007	Ewha Institute for Biomedical Law and Ethics	xenotransplantation

cess. However, in South Korea, civil groups and research institutes took leading roles in the conferences, disconnected from the National Assembly and the government. Because of this, the final reports from the conferences had little effect on policy decisions (Ahn and Kim 2009; Yoon 2005).

Citizens' Juries

In the 1970s, citizen's juries were developed by Ned Crosby, a student writing his doctoral dissertation. He intended to create a process that would enhance reason among citizens as they discussed public policies and politicians. He later founded the Jefferson Center to refine the citizens' juries and has managed many of them or similar democratic processes over the decades to evaluate policy issues and to review candidates in presidential or gubernatorial elections.[2] Around the same period, in Germany, Peter Dienel at the Research Institute for Citizen Participation, University of Wuppertal, initiated a similar democratic process in the name of "planning cells" (Planungzellen; Smith and Wales 2000, 56). The public agencies supported the Research Institute and agreed to consider the recommendations of these planning cells in decision-making processes (Smith and Wales 2000). Inspired by these

---

2 https://jefferson-center.org/our-history/ (assessed March 2020).

practices, numerous citizens' juries have been conducted in many democratic countries to discuss a variety of policy issues.

Citizen juries were held in South Korea several times by multiple organizations. Among them, the Ulsan Buk-gu case in 2004 is one of the most well-known. In 2002, the Buk-gu government made a plan to build a food waste recycling facility at Jungsan-dong and attempted to construct it in 2003 after the Buk-gu council approved it. However, residents of Jungsan-dong strongly opposed and protested against its construction. In 2004, a six-member committee organized by the Democratic Labor Party arbitrated the dispute, and a delegation of the residents agreed with the government that a citizen jury would determine whether the food waste recycling facility was allowed to be constructed at Jungsan-dong. Local residents then approved this agreement through a referendum (Kim 2006; Jeong 2011).

At first, NGOs and religious groups in Ulsan recommended jury candidates, and forty-three people among them were selected as jury members. Then, they visited the site where a food waste recycling facility would be built, and had public hearings and meetings to discuss whether to approve the construction of the facility and how to resolve some legal issues between the construction company and local residents. Finally, on December 28, 2004, the citizen jury decided to construct the facility. Among thirty-nine jurors who participated in voting, thirty-one favored the constriction, while nine disfavored it, and one ballot was voided (Kim 2006).

Following this decision by the citizen jury, the construction of the food waste recycling facility was resumed and completed in 2005. After the facility began operation, however, bad smells began emanating from it. Since this fact broke the promise of Buk-gu government, local residents submitted a petition and began a signature-seeking campaign to stop the operation of the facility. Only one year after the citizen jury approved the construction of the facility, the operation was suspended, public hearings were held, and the facility was finally closed down, wasting more than 2 billion Korean won (about $ 1.7 million USD) (Jeong 2011).

Deliberative Poll

James S. Fishkin introduced the deliberative poll to make the policy-making process more representative, thoughtful, and reasonable (Fishkin 1995). The typical process of a deliberative poll is as follows. First, select hundreds of people through random probabilistic extraction methods and make them stay in a single place for several days. Then immerse the participants in policy issues, with carefully balanced briefing materials, small-group discussions, and Q&A sessions with competing experts, interest groups, and politicians who have different views on the issues. Then, on the final day of deliberation, poll the participants in detail. Finally, based on those survey results, a final report should be written and delivered to policymakers who will make a decision with respect to that issue (Fishkin 1995, 162).

In 1994, the deliberative poll was initially implemented in Manchester, England to discuss the issue of rising crime and what to do about it. It was then soon adopted at the national issues conference, which was held at the University of Texas at Austin, to deal with several key issues of the 1996 U.S. presidential election (Luskin et al. 2002; Fishkin 1995). Since then, many national and local governments have used deliberative polls to review various policy issues.

In the 2017 presidential election in South Korea, Moon Jae-in pledged to halt construction on Shin-Gori Nuclear Reactors No. 5 and 6. After he was elected as president, the construction of the nuclear reactors was suspended. As of late May 2017, however, considerable progress has been made on the construction since the government permit was issued in 2016, and it proved difficult for the president to cancel the constriction. A huge amount of money was already spent, and additional costs were expected to be incurred, if the construction was halted. Thus, President Moon decided to submit this issue to a public deliberation process and promised to follow whatever decision was reached (The Public Deliberation Committee 2017, 16-17). Followed by his order, The Public Deliberation Committee on Shin-Gori Nuclear Reactors No. 5 & 6 was composed of nine members and officially launched on July 24, 2017 (The Public Deliberation Committee 2017, 17-19).

To select participants to take part in the public deliberation, a method of double sampling for stratification was employed in the following way. Korean citizens over 19 years of age were stratified three-dimensionally by region, gender, and age group. A proportionally distributed group of approximately 20,000 was selected by employing random sampling to form an initial sample group. It was then stratified three-dimensionally by attitude on the resumption of the Shin-Gori Nuclear Reactors (support, opposition, not decided yet), gender, and age group to produce a proportionally distributed group of 500 by random sampling (The Public Deliberation Committee 2017, 33-34).

An orientation to the public deliberation was held on September 16, 2017. Five hundred people, as described above, were invited, and a total of 478 people eventually attended the orientation (The Public Deliberation Committee 2017, 35-36). For them, a deliberation sourcebook including critical information on the public deliberation process, nuclear energy, and the Shin-Gori Nuclear Reactors was mailed, and the e-learning system was provided to promote understanding of the issue through video lectures showing the pros and cons of the nuclear reactors and to answer members' questions in September and October (The Public Deliberation Committee 2017, 37-39).

After that, the deliberative forum was held at Kyesongwon in Cheonan from October 13 to 15, 2017. A total of 471 of the 478 attendees at the orientation were present, while seven declined to participate for personal reasons. The deliberative forum consisted of presentations by export and interest groups for and against the resumption of construction of the nuclear reactors, a small group discussion, a Q&A session, and a comprehensive discussion on the final choice. In addition, two surveys were conducted: one on the first day and one on the final day of the deliberative forum (The Public Deliberation Committee 2017, 39-42). At the final survey, as seen in Table 13-2, 59.5% of the participants were in favor of resuming the construction while 40.5% of them disapproved.

Based on the result, The Public Deliberation Committee recommended that the Korean government resume construction of Shin-Gori Nuclear Reactors. The government accepted the recommendation so that the construction of the nuclear reactors would be restarted in

Table 13-2. The Percentage of Those for and against Resuming the Construction (%)

Survey		For	Against	Undecided
General Survey (20,006 respondents)		36.6	27.6	35.8
Participants in the Public Deliberation	1st	36.6	27.6	35.8
	3rd	44.7	30.7	24.6
	4th	57.2	39.4	3.3
	Final	59.5	40.5	

Note: The second survey did not ask whether respondents approve or disapprove the resumption of the construction. In the fourth survey, the respondents were given only two choices, excluding "undecided".
Source: The Public Deliberation Committee 2017, 87.

2017.3 Public opinion on the outcome of the public deliberation was positive. Even civil and environmental groups, which strongly opposed the resumption of the construction, stated in a press conference that they respected the decision of the participants in the public deliberation.4

4. Conclusion

There is an optimistic view on public deliberation. Not all public deliberation, however, is successful. As seen in the case of the citizen jury in Ulsan, if social conflict on the policy issue is severe, public deliberation may not achieve social consensus because reasoned arguments are almost impossible. In a similar vein, Barabas (2004) showed that strong-minded participants in public deliberation are likely to refuse to accept others' views.

Further, some critics are suspicious of the legitimacy of public deliberation. For example, in the decision on whether to resume the construction of Shin-Gory Nuclear Reactors, they argued that it should be discussed and determined by the National Assembly, a representative body of the general public, and not by a randomly-selected group of participants engaged in public deliberation, given the magnitude of the economic and environmental impacts at the national level.

Finally, the decisions that ordinary citizens make with respect to policy decisions on some complex and technological issues may not be adequate. Sometimes, specialized expertise is required, and therefore experts are more likely to make decisions that reflect a wide range of the issues involved.

---

3 http://www.hani.co.kr/arti/politics/bluehouse/815488.html

4 https://moneys.mt.co.kr/news/mwView.php?no=2017102017098073601&type=&&V MN

References

Abramowitz, Alan I. and Steven Webster. 2016. "The Rise of Negative Partisanship and the Nationalization of U.S. Elections in the 21st Century." *Electoral Studies* 41: 12-22.

Abrams, Dominic, and Michael A. Hogg. 2004. "A social psychological framework for understanding social inclusion and exclusion." In *Social psychology of inclusion and exclusion.* London: Psychology Press.

Accetti, Carlo Invernizzi and Ian Zuckerman. 2017. "What's Wrong with Militant Democracy?" *Political Studies* 65(1S): 182-199.

Achen, Christopher H. and Larry M. Bartels. 2016. *Democracy for Realists: Why Elections Do Not Produce Responsive Government.* Princeton: Princeton University Press.

Ahn, Kyung-Sup and Na-Young Kim. 2009. *Korean Policy Sciences Review* 13(2): 145-174.

Alba, Richard, and Victor Nee. 2003. *Remaking the American Mainstream: Assimilation and Contemporary Immigration.* Cambridge, MA: Harvard University Press.

Allcott, Hunt, and Matthew Gentzkow. 2017. "Social Media and Fake News in the 2016 Election." *Journal of Economic Perspectives* 31(2): 211-236.

Allport, Gordon Willard. 1954. *The Nature of Prejudice. Cambridge* MA: Perseus Books.

Altman, David. 2017. "The Potential of Direct Democracy: A Global Measure (1900-2014)." *Social Indicators Research* 133(3): 1207-1227.

Andersen, Robert, and Tina Fetner. 2008. "Cohort differences in tolerance of homosexuality: Attitudinal change in Canada and the United States, 1981-2000." *Public Opinion Quarterly* 72(2): 311-330.

Baek, Young Min. 2015. "Political mobilization through social network sites: The mobilizing power of political messages received from SNS friends." *Computers in Human Behavior* 44: 12-19.

Bafumi, Joseph, and Robert Y. Shapiro. 2009. "A New Partisan Voter." *Journal of Politics* 71(1): 1-24.

Bakshy, Eytan, Solomon Messing, and Lada A. Adamic. 2015. "Exposure to Ideologically Diverse News and Opinion on Facebook." *Science*: 1130-1132.

Barabas, Jason. 2004. "How Deliberation Affects Policy Opinions." *American Political Science Review* 98(4): 687-701.

Barlow, Fiona Kate, Winnifred R. Louis, and Miles Hewstone. 2009. "Rejected! Cognitions of rejection and intergroup anxiety as mediators of the impact of cross-group friendships on prejudice." *British journal of social psychology* 48(3): 389-405.

Bastos, Marco T., and Dan Mercea. 2019. "The Brexit botnet and user-generated hyperpartisan news." *Social Science Computer Review* 37(1): 38-54.

Belavusau, Uladzislau. 2014. "Hate Speech and Constitutional Democracy in Eastern Europe: Transitional and Militant? (Czech Republic, Hungary and Poland)." *Israel Law Review* 47(1): 27-61.

Bell, Daniel. 2000. *The End of Ideology: On the Exhaustion of Political Ideas in the Fifties*, revised. Cambridge, MA: Harvard University Press.

Bellamy, Richard. 2007. *Political Constitutionalism: A Republican Defence of the Constitutionality of Democracy*. Cambridge: Cambridge University Press.

Berlo, David. 1960. *The Process of Communication*. New York, New York: Rinehart & Winston.

Bessette, Joseph M. 1980. "Deliberative Democracy : the Majority Principle in Republican Government." in Robert A. Goldwin and William A. Schambra (eds.) *How democratic is the constitution?* American Enterprise Institute for Public Policy Research.

Bobo, Lawrence, and Frederick C. Licari. 1989. "Education and political tolerance: Testing the effects of cognitive sophistication and target group affect." *Public Opinion Quarterly* 53(3): 285-308.

Bochsler, Daniel and Simon Hug. 2015. "How Minorities Fare Under Referendums: A Cross-National Study." *Electoral Studies* 38: 206-216.

Bong-woo Nam. 2017. "Hanguk Minjujuui Anjeonghwa Dangye Deureoseossda." *Naeilshinmoon*. Retrieved from http://m.naeil.com/m_news_view.php?id_art=256397

Booth, Paul, Amber L. Davisson, Aaron Hess, and Ashley Hinck. 2018. *Poaching Politics: Online Communication During the 2016 US Presidential Election*. Peter Lang Publishing, Inc.

Boyd, Danah M., and Nicole B. Ellison. 2007. "Social etwork sites: Definition, history, and scholarship." *Journal of Computer-Mediated Communication* 13(1): 210-230.

Boyd, Danah, and Kate Crawford. 2012. "Critical questions for big data: Provocations for a cultural, technological, and scholarly phenomenon." *Information, Communication, and Society* 15(5): 662-679.

Boyd, Danah. 2015. "Social media: A phenomenon to be analyzed." *Social Media & Society* 1(1). Retrieved from http://doi.org./10.1177/2056305115580148

Bradshaw, Samantha, and Philip N. Howard. 2017. "Troops, Trolls and Troublemakers: A Global Inventory of Social Media Manipulation." *Computational Propaganda Project Working Paper*.

Brundidge, Jennifer. 2010. "Encountering "difference" in the contemporary public sphere: The contribution of the Internet to the heterogeneity of political discussion networks." *Journal of Communication* 60(4): 680-700.

Bugarič, Bojan. 2019. "Central Europe's descent into autocracy: A constitutional analysis of authoritarian populism." *International Journal of Constitutional Law* 17(2): 597-616.

Burchardt, Tania, Julian Le Grand, and David Piachaud. 1999. "Social exclusion in Britain 1991—1995." *Social policy & administration* 33(3): 227-244.

Cacioppo, John. T., Wendy L. Gardener, and Gary G. Berntson. 1997. "Beyond Bipolar Conceptualizations and Measures: The Case of Attitudes and Evaluative Space." *Personality and Social Psychology Review* 1: 3-25.

Cadwalladr, Carole, and Emma Graham-Harrison. 2018. "Revealed: 50 million Facebook profiles harvested for Cambridge Analytica in major data breach." *The Guardian* 17:22 Retrieved from https://www.theguardian.com/news/2018/mar/17/cambridge-analytica-facebook-influence-us-election

Cameron, Angus. 2006. "Geographies of welfare and exclusion: social inclusion and exception." *Progress in Human Geography* 30(3): 396-404.

Castles, Stephen, Mark J. Miller, and Giuseppe Ammendola. 2013. *The age of migration: International population movements in the modern world.* New York: Guilford Press.

Chaffee, Steven H. 1975. "Political Communication: Issues and Strategies for Research." *Sage Annual Reviews of Communication* Volume IV. Beverly Hills, California, Sage Publications

Chambers, Simone. 2003. "Deliberative Democratic Theory." *Annual Review of Political Science* 8: 307-326.

Cheon, Byung-You & Jin Wook Shin. 2014. "Are Low-Incomes More Likely to be Politically Conservative? Party Support and Policy Attitudes by Income in South Korea, 2003-2012" *Journal of Korean Social Trend and Perspective* 11: 9-52.

Cheon, Byung-You, Jiyeun Hwang, Gyu Seoung Shin, Jin Wook Kang, Shin Wook Lee, Byung Hee Kim, Hyun Joo. 2013. "Growing Inequality and Its Impacts in Korea" *GINI Country Report Korea.* (January 2013)

Child, Jeffrey T., and Sandra Petronio. 2011. "Unpackiing the Paradoxes of Privacy in CMC Relationships: The Challenges of Blogging and Relational Communication on the Internet. In K. B. Wright & L. M. Webb (Eds.), *Computer-Mediated Communication in Personal Relationships* (pp. 21-40). New York: Peter Lang.

Child, Jeffrey T., Judy C. Pearson, and Sandra Petronio. 2009. "Blogging, Communication, and Privacy Management: Development of the blogging privacy management measure." *Journal of the American Society for Information Science and Technology* 60: 2079-2094.

Cho, Hyun-Ju 2018. "AI interviewers promise unbiased hiring." *Korea Joongang Daily.* Retrieved from http://koreajoongangdaily.joins.com/news/article/article.aspx?aid=3045827

Cho, Hyun-Yun and Cheong-Seok. 2016. "Pluralistic two nation strategy of the Park Geun-hye administration and generation conflict -focusing on public officials pension and salary peak." *Economy and Society* 110: 70-299.

Cho, Jinman, Jongbin Yoon, Sangjoon Ka, and Sung-jin Yoo. 2011. "The Perceptual Gap on Political Tolerance between the Winners and the Losers and Its Effects." *Journal of Korean Politics* 20(2): 29-51.

Cho, Youngho, Mi-son Kim, and Yong Cheol Kim. 2019. "Cultural Foundations of Contentious Democracy in South Korea: What Type of Democracy Do Korean Citizens Prefer?" *Asian Survey* 59(2): 272-294.

Choe, Hyun. 2007. " National Identity and Multicultural Citizenship in South Korea." *Civil Society and NGO* 5(2): 147-173.

Choi, Jang-jip. 1988. *Labor Movements and the State in South Korea.* Seoul: Yeolum.

Choi, Jang-jip. 2006. *Democracy after Democratization.* Seoul: Humanitas. (in Korean)

Chun Sangchin. 2018. *The Generation Game: beyond 'Generation Frames'.* Seoul: Moonji Publishing:.

Chun, Sangchin. 2004. "The Poverty of the Generational Research: A Study on the Generation Research Methodology." *Korean Journal of Sociology* 38 (5): 31-52.

Cole, Alexandra. 2005. "Old Right or New Right? The Ideological Positioning of Parties of the Far Right." *European Journal of Political Research* 44: 203-30.

Corak, Miles. 2013. "Income Inequality, Equality of Opportunity, and Intergenerational Mobility." *Journal of Economic Perspectives* 27(3), 79-102.

Côté, Rochelle R., and Bonnie H. Erickson. 2009. "Untangling the roots of tolerance: How forms of social capital shape attitudes toward ethnic minorities and immigrants." *American Behavioral Scientist* 52(12): 1664-1689.

Dalton, Russell J. 2007. "Partisan Mobilization, Cognitive Mobilization and the Changing American Electorate." *Electoral Studies* 26: 274-86.

Daly, Eoin. 2015. "A Republican Defence of The Constitutional Referendum." *Legal Studies* 35(1): 30-54.

Datta, Amit, Michael Carl Tschantz, and Anupam Datta. 2015. "Automated experiments on ad privacy settings." *Proceedings on Privacy Enhancing Technologies* 2015(1): 92-112.

Davis, Tom, Martin Frost, and Richard Cohen. 2014. *The Partisan Divide: Congress in Crisis.* Campbell, CA: Premiere.

Davis, Warren W. 2007. *Negative Liberty: Public Opinion and the Terrorist Attacks on*

America. New York: Russell Sage Foundation.

Deli Carpini, Michael X., Fay Lomax Cook, and Lawrence R. Jacobs. 2004. "Public Deliberation, Discursive Participation, and Citizen Engagement: A Review of the Empirical Literature." *Annual Review of Political Science* 7: 315-344.

Diakopoulos, Nicholas. 2015. "Algorithmic accountability: Journalistic investigation of computational power structures." *Digital journalism* 3(3): 398-415.

Dixon, Jeffrey C., and Michael S. Rosenbaum. 2004. "Nice to know you? Testing contact, cultural, and group threat theories of anti-Black and anti-Hispanic stereotypes." *Social Science Quarterly* 85(2): 257-280.

Dobrota, Marina, Veljko Jeremic, and Aleksandar Markovic. 2012. "A new perspective on the ICT Development Index." *Information Development* 28(4): 271-280.

Dovidio, John. F., Gaertner, Samuel, L., Hodson, Gordon, and Houlette, Melissa. A, and Johnson Kelly, M. 2004. "Social inclusion and exclusion: Recategorization and the perception of intergroup boundaries." In *Social psychology of inclusion and exclusion*. London: Psychology Press.

Dryzek, John S., and Aviezer Tucker. 2008. "Deliberative innovation to different effect: Consensus conferences in Denmark, France, and the United States." *Public Administration Review* 68(5): 864-876.

Dryzek, John. 2000. *Deliberative Democracy and beyond Liberals, Critics, Contestations*. New York : Oxford University Press.

Dutton, Tim, Brent Barron, and Gaga Boskovic. 2018. "Building an AI World" *Report on National and Regional AI Strategies*. Toronto: CIFAR.

Einsiedel, Edna F., and Deborah L. Eastlick. 2000. "Consensus Conferences as Deliberative Democracy: A Communications Perspective." *Science Communication* 21(4): 323-343.

Eischen, Kyle. 2003. "Opening the 'Black Box'of Software The micro-foundations of informational technologies, practices and environments." *Information, Communication & Society* 6(1): 57-81.

Ely, John Hart. 1980. *Democracy and Distrust: A Theory of Judicial Review*. Cambridge, MA: Harvard University Press.

Esses, Victoria, M., Dovidio, John, F., Jackson, Lynne, M., and Armstrong, Tamara, L. 2001. "The immigration dilemma: The role of perceived group competition, ethnic prejudice, and national identity." *Journal of Social issues* 57(3): 389-412.

Evans, Geoffrey and Stephen Whitefield. 1999. "The Emergence of Class Politics and Class Voting in Post-Communist Russia." In *The End of Class Voting? Class Voting in Comparative Context.* Ed. Geoffrey Evans. Oxford: Oxford University Press, 254-278.

Findlay Stephanie, Schipani Andres and Murgia Madhumita. 2019. "India: The WhatsApp election." Financial Times, 5 May. Available at: www.ft.com/content/9fe88fba-6c0d-11e9-a9a5-351eeaef6d84

Fink, Katherine. 2018. "Opening the government's black boxes: freedom of information and algorithmic accountability." *Information, Communication & Society* 21(10): 1453-1471.

Fishkin, James S. 1995. *The Voice of the People: Public Opinion and Democracy.* New Haven, CT: Yale University Press.

Franklin, Mark N., Thomas T. Mackie and Henry Valen. 1992. *Electoral Change: Responses to Evolving Social and Attitudinal Structures in Western Countries.* Cambridge; New York: Cambridge University Press.

Freitag, M., and M. Bühlmann. 2009. "Crafting Trust: The Role of Political Institutions in a Comparative Perspective." *Comparative Political Studies* 42(12): 1537-1566.

Fuchs, Christian. 2014. *Social Media: A Critical Introduction.* Thousand Oaks, CA: SAGE.

Funk, Carolyn L. 2000. "The dual influence of self-interest and societal interest in public opinion." *Political Research Quarterly* 53(1): 37-62.

Gerbaudo, Paolo. 2019a. *The Digital Party: Political Organisation and Online Democracy.* Pluto Press.

Gerbaudo, Paolo. 2019b. "Are digital parties more democratic than traditional parties? Evaluating Podemos and Movimento 5 Stelle's online decision-making platforms." Party Politics DOI: 10.1177/1354068819884878

Gibson, James L. 2008." Intolerance and Political Repression in the United States: A Half-century after McCarthyism." *American Journal of Political Science* 52: 96-108.

Gibson, James L. 2013. "Measuring Political Tolerance and General Support for Pro-civil Liberties Policies." *Public Opinion Quarterly* 77: 45-68.

Gibson, James L., and Richard D. Bingham. 1982. "On the conceptualization and measurement of political tolerance." *American Political Science Review* 76(3): 603-620.

Gordon, Milton M. 1964. *Assimilation in American Life: The Role of Race, Religion, and National Origin.* New York: Oxford University Press.

Habermas, Jürgen. 1996. *Between Facts and Norms: Contributions to a Discourse Theory of Law and Democracy.* Cambridge, MA: MIT Press.

Hadler, Markus. 2012. "The influence of world societal forces on social tolerance. A time comparative study of prejudices in 32 countries." *The Sociological Quarterly* 53(2): 211-237.

Haider-Markel, Donald P. 2010. *Out and running: Gay and lesbian candidates, elections, and policy representation.* Washington D. C.: Georgetown University Press.

Han, Guiyoung. 2013. "Why Did the Poor Vote to the Conservative Party in 2012 President Election?" *Journal of Korean Social Trend and Perspective* 10: 9-40.

Hayes, Alan, Matthew Gray, and Ben Edwards. 2008. *Social inclusion. Origin, concepts and key themes.* Canberra: Social Inclusion Unit, Department of the Prime Minister and Cabinet.

Heide, Brandon Van Der, Jonathan D. D'Angelo, and Erin M. Schumaker. 2012. "The Effects of Verbal versus Photographic Self-presentation on Impression Formation in Facebook." *Journal of Communication* 62: 98-116.

Helmond, Anne.. 2015. "The Platformization of the Web: Making Web Data Platform Ready." *Social Media & Society* 1(2). DOI: 10.1177/2056305115603080

Hewstone, Miles, Cairns, Ed, Voci, Alberto, Paolini, Stefania, McLernon, Frances, Crisp, Richard. J., Niens, Ulrike, and Craig, Jean. 2005. "Intergroup contact in a divided society: Challenging segregation in Northern Ireland." *In The social psychology of inclusion and exclusion.* New York: Psychology Press.

Hjerm, M. 1998. "National Identities, National Pride and Xenophobia: A Comparison of Four Western Countries." *Act Sociological* 41(4): 335-347.

Hjerm, M. 2005. "What the Future May Bring: Xenophobia among Swedish Adolescents." *Acta Sociologica* 48(4): 292-307.

Holmes, Aaron. 2020. "Facebook knows what you're doing on other sites and in real life. This tool lets you see what it knows about you." *Business Insider*. Retrieved from https://www.businessinsider.com/facebook-clear-history-offline-activity-tracker-tool-how-to-use-2020-1

Hong, Seong-Ku. 2011. "Theoretical complementation of deliberative democracy: With focus on republican-oriented alternative]." *Media & Society* 19(2): 152-184.

Hong, Young Ran et al. 2015. "Generational Conflicts Covered in Media and Their Implication." KEDI Position Paper 2015-03.

Hovland, Carl Iver, Irving Lester Janis, and Harold H. Kelley. 1953. *Communication and Persuasion*. New Haven: Yale University Press.

Howell, S., and D. Fagan. 1988. "Race and Trust in Government: Testing the Political Reality Model." *Public Opinion Quarterly* 52: 343-350.

Huddy, Leonie, Lilliana Mason, and Lene Aaroe. 2015. "Expressive Partisanship: Campaign Involvement, Political Emotion, and Partisan Identity." *American Political Science Review* 109(1): 1-17.

Huddy, Leonie, S. Feldman, C. Taber, and G. Lahav. 2005. "Threat, Anxiety, and Support of Antiterrorism Policies." *American Journal of Political Science* 49: 593-608.

Huntington, Samuel P. 1991. "Democracy's Third Wave." *Journal of Democracy* 2(2): 12-34.

Hur, Suk Jae. 2019. "Changing Regional Voting Behavior of Korean Voters." *Journal of Contemporary Politics* 12(2): 5-37.

HUSAFIK: Headquarters United States Army Military Government in Korea, Department of Public Information, Seoul, Korea, Washington National Record Center, Suitland, Md (1991. VI) In Shin, Bok-Ryong eds. The Collections of Korean Division History. Wonju-moon-wha-sa.

Hwang, Yong-suk, and Kim, Ki-Tae. 2019. "The survey of recommendation system research trends and methods." *Journal of Cybercommunication* 36(2): 221-253.

Im, Jaehyung and Jaesin Kim. 2015. "An Empirical Analysis on the Disliked Group and Tolerance in Korea." *OUGHTOPIA* 30(2): 273-98.

International Organization for Migration. 2011. *Glossary on Migration. 2nd edn.*

Geneva: Switzerland.

Isenberg, Daniel J. 1986. "Group polarization: A critical review and meta -analysis." *Journal of Personality and Social Psychology* 50(6): 1141-1151.

Isike, Efe Mary. 2017. "A Contact Theory Analysis of South Africans' Perceptions of Nigerian Immigration." *African Population Studies* 31(1): 3225-3233.

Islam, Mir Rabiul, and Miles Hewstone. 1993. "Dimensions of contact as predictors of intergroup anxiety, perceived out-group variability, and out-group attitude: An integrative model." *Personality and Social Psychology Bulletin* 19(6): 700-710.

Iyengar, Shanto, Gaurav Sood, and Yphtach Lelkes. 2012. "Affect, Not Ideology: A Social Identity Perspective on Polarization." *Public Opinion Quarterly* 76(3): 405-31.

Iyengar, Shanto, Yphtach Lelkes, Matthew Levendusky, Neil Malhotra, and Sean J. Westwood. 2019. "The Origins and Consequences of Affective Polarization in the United States." *Annual Review of Political Science* 22: 129-146.

Iyengar, Shanto, Yphtach Lelkes, Matthew Levendusky, Neil Malhotra, and Sean J Westwood. 2019. "The Origins and Consequences of Affective Polarization in the United States." *Annual Review of Political Science* 22: 129-146.

James Vincent. 2017. "Yep, human workers are listening to recordings from Google Assistant, too." *The Verge*. Retrieved from https://www.theverge. com/2019/7/11/20690020/google-assistant-home-human-contractors-listening-recordings-vrt-nws

Janda, Kenneth. 1980. *Political Parties: A Cross-National Survey*. New York: The Free Press.

Jang, Seung-Jin and JeongKyu Suh. 2019. "Dual Structures of Partisan Polarization in the Korean Electorate: Political Identity, Issue Preferences, Political Sophistication." *Korean Party Studies Review* 18(3): 5-29.

Jang, Seung-jin. 2013. "The 2012 Elections and the Possibility (and Limitation) of Class Cleavage" *Korean Political Science Review* 47(4): 51-70.

Jang, Woonsok. 2019. *The Lawmaker's Perception on the Political Video Channels of YouTube and the Impact on the Political Socialization of the Electorate*. Doctoral Dissertation.

Jeon, Yongjoo. 2005. "Democratization of Candidate Selection in Korean Parties and

Its Implication: A Case Study on the 17th General Election of 2004 in Korea."
Korean Political Science Review 39(2): 217-236.

Jeong, Hoi Ok. 2013. "Do National Feelings Influence Public Attitudes towards
Immigration?" *Journal of Ethnic and Migration Studies* 39: 1461-1477.

Jeong, Hoi Ok. 2016. "A New Typology of Perceived Discrimination and Its
Relationship to Immigrants' Political Trust." *Polish Sociological Review* 194:
209-226.

Jeong, Jeong Hwa. "Public Conflict and Consensus Building: The Application
and Limitations of Deliberative Democracy" *Korean Public Administration
Quarterly* 23(2): 577-606.

Jones, David R. 2010. "Partisan Polarization and Congressional Accountability in
House Elections." *American Journal of Political Science* 54(2): 323-37.

Jones, F. L. and Smith, F. 2001. "Individual and Societal Bases of National Identity: a
Comparative Multilevel Analysis." *European Sociological Review* 17(2): 103-118.

Joppke, C., and E. Morawska (Ed.). 2003. *Toward Assimilation and Citizenship
Immigrants in Liberal Nation-States*. Basing-Stoke: Palgrave Macmillan.

Jung, Dong-Joon, Sun Kim, Heejung Kim, Yong-woo Na, Inchul Mun, Young Hoon
Song, Gyubin Choi, Kyung Hoon Leem and Jungok Lee. 2018. *The 2018
Unification Perception Survey*. Seoul National University.

Jung, Dong-Joon. 2017. "South Korea's Ideological Congruence between Citizens
and Representatives: Conceptualization and Measurement." *Legislative Studies*
23(2): 67-108.

Jung, Dong-Joon. 2018. "Political Polarization among South Korean Citizens after the
2018 Local Elections: The Rise of Partisan Sorting and Negative Partisanship."
OUGHTOPIA 33(3): 143-180.

Jung, Dong-Joon. 2020a. "A Theoretical Review on the Crisis of Democracy:
Focusing on Referendums, Judicial Review, and Party Bans." *Journal of
Contemporary Politics* 13(1): 79-115.

Jung, Dong-Joon. 2020b. "In the Name of "The People"? Between Irresponsible
Bipartisanship and Responsible Partisanship." in Opinion, CFPS Webzine *On
Mirae* 1.

Jung, Hae Sik et al. 2018. "A Study of Social Problem and Social Cohesion in Korea with Policy Recommendations (V)." KIHASA Report 2018-30.

Jung, Hyun Tae & Yun-Sou Oh. 2009. "Korean Welfare Policies and the Ideology and Mindset of the Korean People Based on John Rawls' Theory of Justice." *Social Welfare Policy* 36 (1), 329-353.

Ka, Sang Joon. 2014. "Has the Korean National Assembly been polarized?" *Journal of Parliamentary Research* 9(2): 247-272.

Ka, Sang Joon. 2016. "Policy Attitude of Legislators and Polarization of the National Assembly." *OUGHTOPIA* 31(1): 327-354.

Ka, Sangjoon, Jongbin Yoo, and Sung-jin Yoo. 2010. "An Study on Political Tolerance in Korea and Its Determinants." *OUGHTOPI* 25(3): 273-298.

Ka, Sangjoon. 2015. "A Study on Political Tolerance of Korean Society: Low tolerance and Deep conflict." *Korean Party Studies Review* 14(1): 129-155.

Ka, Sangjoon. 2016. "Political Tolerance and Attitude on disliked groups." *East and West Studies* 28(3): 1-24.

Kääriäinen, J. T. 2007. "Trust in Police in 16 European Countries: A Multilevel Analysis." *European Journal of Criminology* 4(4): 409-435.

Kaid, Lynda Lee, ed. 2004. *Handbook of Political Communication Research*. Mahwah, NJ: Lawrence Erlbaum Associates, Inc.

Kang, Won-Taek. 2012. "Ideological Positions and Policy Attitudes of the 19th National Assembly of Korea." *Legislative Studies* 18(2): 5-38.

Kang, Won-Taek. 2015. "The Political Party Act and Its Impacts on Party Politics in South Korea." *Korean Party Studies Review* 14(2): 5-32.

Kang, Won-Taek. 2018. *Understanding Korean Politics*. Seoul: Pakyoungsa.

Kang, Won Take. 1998. "The Rise of a Third Party in South Korea: the Unification National Party in the 1992 National Assembly Election" *Electoral Studies* 17(1): 95-110.

Kang, Woo Jin. 2012. "The Political Consequence of Citizens' Perceptions of Economic Inequality in Korea: Focusing on its Effect on the Efficacy of Democracy." *Korea and International Politics* 77: 145-175.

Karp, Jeffrey A. And Susan A. Banducci. 2007. "Party Mobilization and Political Participation in New and Old Democracies." *Party Politics* 13(2): 217-234.

Katz, Richard S. 2001. "The Problem of Candidate Selection and Models of Party

Democracy." *Party Politics* 7(3): 277-296.

Kaufmann, Bruno, Rolf Büchi and Nadja Braun. 2010. *Guidebook to Direct Democracy in Switzerland and Beyond.* The Initiative & Referendum Institute Europe.

Kelsen, Hans. 2006. *General Theory of Law and State.* London: Transaction Publishers.

Kevins, Anthony, and Stuart N. Soroka. 2018. "Growing Apart? Partisan Sorting in Canada, 1992-2015." *Canadian Journal of Political Science* 51(1): 103-33.

Kim, Hansung, Sooyeon Huh, Sangmi Choi, & Yushin Lee. 2018. "Perceptions of Inequality and Attitudes towards Redistribution in Four East Asian Welfare States." *International Journal of Social Welfare* 27: 28-39.

Kim, Hee Min, Jun Young Choi, & Jinman Cho. 2008. "Changing Cleavage Structure in New Democracies: An Empirical Analysis of Political Cleavages in Korea." *Electoral Studies* 27(1): 136-150.

Kim, Hisam. 2014. Intergenerational Mobility and the Role of Education in Korea." Korean Development Institute (KDI) Workshop on Human Capital Policy, Seoul (Oct. 6. 2014).

Kim, Jiyoon, Chungku Kang and Kildong Kim. 2018. "U.S.-North Korea Summit and South Koreans Perceptions of Neighboring Countries." *ASAN Institute for Policy Studies.*

Kim, Jiyoon, Chungku Kang, and Eui Chul Lee. 2014. *Korea Closed: Koreans' multicultural awareness and policy.* Issue Brief 2014(4).

Kim, Man-Heum. 1995. "Political Cleavages, Party Politics, and Localism in Korea." *Korean Political Science Review* 28(2): 215-237.

Kim, So Yeon. 2006. "A successful Consensus Model? - Assessment and its Implication of the Civil Jury in Ulsan, Korea." *Civil Society and NGO* 4(2): 175-205.

Kim, Sonho and Kim, Weekhun. 2019 "Up-rise of YouTube in Korea: Partial Results of Digital News Report 2019." *Media Issue* 5(3). Korea Press Foundation.

Kim, Wonik. 2010. "Does Class Matter? Social Cleavages in South Korea's Electoral Politics in the Era of Neoliberalism." *Review of Political Economy* 22(4): 589-616.

Kim, Yong Cheol, Youngho Cho, & Jungsub Shin. 2018. "Class Consciousness in South Korea in the Age of Neoliberalism: The Effects of Socioeconomic Conditions and Subjective Social Stratification Recognition on Class Consciousness." *OUGHTOPIA* 33(1): 99-134.

Kim, Yong Cheol. 2017. *Labor Politics in South Korea: Change and Dynamics*. Paju: Mind Tap.

Kim, Yonghwan. 2011. The contribution of social network sites to exposure to political difference: The relationships among SNSs, online political messaging, and exposure to cross-cutting perspectives. *Computers in Human Behavior* 27: 971-977.

Koene, Ansgar, Clifton, Chris, Hatada, Yohko, Webb, Helena, and Richardson, Rashida. 2019. "A governance framework for algorithmic accountability and transparency." *European Parliamentary Research Service*. 1-107.

Koev, Dan. 2015. "Interactive party effects on electoral performance: How ethnic minority parties aid the populist right in Central and Eastern Europe." *Party Politics* 21(4): 649-659.

Koo, Hagen. 2007. "The Changing Faces of Inequality in South Korea in the Age of Globalization." *Korean Studies* 31: 1-18.

Korea Land and Housing Corporation. 2019. *Statistics of Urban Planning (2018)*. http://kosis.kr/statHtml/statHtml.do?orgId=315&tblId=TX_315_2009_H1009

Kreps, David, and Kai Kimppa. 2015. "Theorizing web 3.0: ICTs in a changing society." *Information Technology & People* 28: 726-741.

Kretschmer, Martin, George Michael Klimis, and Roger Wallis. 2001. "Music in electronic markets: An empirical study." *New Media & Society 3*: 417-441.

Kreuzer, Marcus and Vello Pettai. 2009. "Party Switching, Party Systems, and Political Representation." in William B. Heller and Carol Mershon eds. *Political Parties and Legislative Party Switching*. New York: Palgrave MacMillan. 265-285.

Kurlantzick, Joshua. 2014. *Democracy in Retreat: The Revolt of the Middle Class and the Worldwide Decline of Representative Government*. Yale University Press.

Kwon, K. Hazel, Shin-Il Moon, and Michael A. Stefanone. 2015. "Unspeaking on

Facebook? Testing network effects on self-censorship of political expressions in social networking sites." *Quality & Quantity* 29: 1417-1435.

Lawrence, David G. 1976. "Procedural Norms and Tolerance: A Reassessment." *American Political Science Review* 70: 80-100.

Lazer, David M, Baum Matthew A, Benkler Yochai, Berinsky AaJ, Greenhill KM, Menczer F, Metzger MJ, Nyhan

Lazer, David M.J, Matthew A. Baum, Yochai Benkler, Adam J. Berinsky, Kelly M. Greenhill, Filippo Menczer, Miriam J. Metzger, Brendan Nyhan, Gordon Pennycook, David Rothschild, Michael Schudson, Steven A. Sloman, Cass R. Sunstein, Emily A. Thorson, Duncan J. Watts, and Jonathan L. Zittrain. 2018. "The Science of Fake News." *Science* 359(6380): 1094-1096.

Lee, Angela Y. 2001. "The Mere Exposure Effect: An Uncertainty Reduction Explanation Revisited". *Personality and Social Psychology Bulletin* 27: 1255-1266.

Lee, Cheol-Sung. 2019. The Generation of Inequality. Seoul: Moonji Publishing.

Lee, Francis LF. 2014. ""Tolerated one way but not the other": Levels and determinants of social and political tolerance in Hong Kong." *Social Indicators Research* 118(2): 711-727.

Lee, Hoon, Nojin Kwak, Scott W. Campbell, and Rich Ling. 2014. "Mobile communication and political participation in South Korea: Examining the intersections between informational and relational uses." *Computers in Human Behavior* 38: 85-92.

Lee, Jae-Kyung and Ji-Yeon Jang. 2015. "Generational Inequality and Generational Politics." *Democratic Society and Policy Studies* 28: 15-44.

Lee, Jae Kyung. 2018. "Aspect and cause of generational conflicts, and a exploring for alternative dispute resolution: Mainly on the rent-seeking society in Korea." *Economy and Society* 118: 18-48.

Lee, Jae Mook. 2019. "A Generational Change of Voters and the Future of Political Parties in Korea: An Exploratory Study." *Journal of Future Politics* 19(2): 5-33.

Lee, Jeong-Jin. 2019. "*A Study on the Candidate Selection and Party Members.*" *Journal of Future Politics* 9(1): 31-60.

Lee, Jin Ock. 2017. "Gender Politics in the Presidential Election: Dis/continuities between the 18th and 19th Presidential Election." *Journals of Womens Studies* 27(2): 95-137.

Lee, Kap-Yun, Jiho Lee, and Sekeol Kim. 2013. "Property Effects on Class Consciousness and Voting in Korea." *Journal of Korean Politics* 22(2): 1-25.

Lee, Nae-Young and Han-Wool Jeong. 2013. "Disaggregating the Generational Cleavage: Cohort Effect and Aging Effect." *Journal of Legislative Studies.* 19(3): 37-83.

Lee, Sang-Woo. 2011. "Immigrants' Political Participation in Multi-Cultural Society." Korean *Journal of Political Science* 19(2): 57-83.

Lee, Young-Hee. 2008. "Consensus Conference as a Project for Democratization of Science and Technology: Korean Experiences." *Journal of Korean Social Trends and Perspectives* 73: 294-324.

Leipziger, Danny M., David Dollar, Anthony F. Shorrocks, and Su-Yong Song. 1992. *The Distribution of Income and Wealth in Korea.* Washington, DC: The World Bank.

Lenta, Patrick. 2004. "Democracy, Rights Disagreements And Judicial Review." *South African Journal on Human Rights* 20(1): 1-31.

Levendusky, Matthew. 2009. *The Partisan Sort: How Liberals Became Democrats and Conservatives Became Republicans.* Chicago, IL: University of Chicago Press.

Lever, Annabelle. 2009. "Democracy and Judicial Review: Are They Really Incompatible?" *Perspectives on Politics* 7(4): 805-822.

Levitsky, Steven and Daniel Ziblatt. 2018. *How Democracies Die.* New York: Crown.

Lim, Jaehyoung, and Jaeshin Kim. 2014. "An Empirical Analysis of Disliked Groups and Tolerance in Korean Society." *The Journal of Social Paradigm Studies* 29(1): 149-174.

Linz, Juan and Alfred Stepan. 1996. *Problems of Democratic Transition and Consolidation: Southern Europe, South America, and Post-Communist Europe.* Baltimore: Johns Hopkins University Press.

Linz, Juan. 1978. "Crisis, Breakdown, and Reequalibration." In *The Breakdown of Democratic Regimes,* ed. Juan Linz and Alfred Stepan. Baltimore: Johns Hopkins University Press, Part I, 1-97.

Lipset, Seymore M. and Stein Rokkan. 1967. *Party Systems and Voter Alignments:*

Cross-National Perspectives. New York: Free Press.

Mallen, Ana, and María Pilar García-Guadilla. 2017. *Venezuela's Polarized Politics: The Paradox of Direct Democracy under Chávez.* Boulder, CO: Lynne Rienner Publishers.

Marquart-Pyatt, S., & Paxton, P. 2007. "In principle and in practice: Learning political tolerance in Eastern and Western Europe." *Political Behavior* 29(1): 89-113.

Marquart-Pyatt, Sandra and Pamela Paxton. 2007. "In Principle and In Practice: Learning Political Tolerance in Eastern and Western Europe." *Political Behavior* 29: 89-113.

Marwick, Alice, and Rebecca Lewis. 2017. "Media manipulation and disinformation online." *New York: Data & Society Research Institute.*

Mason, Lilliana. 2015. ""I Disrespectfully Agree": The Differential Effects of Partisan Sorting On Social and Issue Polarization." *American Journal of Political Science* 59(1): 128-45.

Mason, Lilliana. 2018. *Uncivil Agreement: How Politics Became Our Identity.* University of Chicago Press.

Maxwell, Rahsaan. 2008. "Assimilation, Expectations, and Attitudes: How Ethnic Minority Migrant Groups Feel About Mainstream Society." *Du Bois Review* 5(2): 387-412.

Maxwell, Rahsaan. 2010. "Evaluating Migrant Integration: Political Attitudes across Generations in Europe." *International Migration Review* 44(1): 25-52.

McCoy, Jennifer, Tahmina Rahman, and Murat Somer. 2018. "Polarization and the Global Crisis of Democracy: Common Patterns, Dynamics, and Pernicious Consequences for Democratic Polities." *American Behavioral Scientist* 62(1): 16-42.

McGhee, Eric, Seth Masket, Boris Shor, Steven Rogers, and Nolan Mccarty. 2014. "A Primary Cause of Partisanship? Nomination Systems and Legislator Ideology." *American Journal of Political Science* 58(2): 337-51.

McLeod, Douglas M., Gerald M. Kosicki, and Jack M. Mcleod. 2009. "Political Communication Effects." In J. Bryant & M. B. Oliver (Eds.), *Media effects: Advances in theory and research* (pp. 228-251). New York, NY: Routledge.

McLuhan, Marshall. 1966. *Understanding media: The extensions of man*. New York: Beacon.

McNair, Brian. 2003. *An Introduction to Political Communication*. London: Routledge.

Meade, Grant. 1993. *A Study on the American Military Government in South Korea*. Seoul: Congdongche (translated in Korean by Ahn, Jong-chul).

Mendelberg, Tali. 2002. "The deliberative citizen: Theory and evidence." *Political Decision Making, Deliberation and Participation* 6(1): 151-193.

Michelson, Melissa R. 2003. "The Corrosive Effect of Acculturation: How Mexican Americans Lose Political Trust." *Social Science Quarterly* 84(4): 918-933.

Mishler, William, and Richard Rose.2005. "What are the Political Consequences of Trust?" *Comparative Political Studies* 38: 1050-1078.

Mitchell, Tom M. 1999. "Machine learning and data mining." *Communications of the ACM* 42(11): 30-36.

Mittelstadt, Brent Daniel, Allo, Patrik, Taddeo, Mariarosaria, Wachter, Sandra, and Floridi, Luciano. 2016. "The ethics of algorithms: Mapping the debate." *Big Data & Society* 3(2): 1-21.

Mittelstadt, Brent. 2017. "From individual to group privacy in big data analytics." *Philosophy & Technology* 30(4): 475-494.

Mo, Jongryn and Yongjoo Jeon. 2004. "Primary Elections, Candidate Competitiveness, and the Democratization of Political Parties: A Case Study on the Korean Local Election of 2002." *Korean Political Science Review* 38(1): 233-253.

Montgomery, Stuart. 2019. "What's in an algorithm?: The problem of the black box." *Tufts Observer*. Retrieved from https://tuftsobserver.org/whats-in-an-algorithm-the-problem-of-the-black-box/

Moon, Shin-Il, George A. Barnett, and Yon Soo Lim. 2010. "The structure of international music flows using network analysis." *New Media & Society* 12: 379-399.

Moon, Shin-il, Hyunjoo Lee, and Yon Soo Lim. 2018. "Watching or Being Watched in the Context of SNS Use: Exploring the Relationships between Motivations for Self-Presentation and Voyeurism, and Communication Privacy Management." *International Telecommunications Policy Review* 25: 57-77.

Moon, Woojin. 2016. "Continuity and Change in Ideological Conflict in Korean Electoral Competition: An Analysis of the Cumulative Data Set Since the 15th Presidential Election." *Korean Party Studies Review* 15(3): 37-60.

Moon, Woojin. 2017. "Deactivated Income-based Voting in South Korea: A Theoretical Model and Empirical Data Analyses." *Korean Political Science Review* 51(4): 101-122.

Moon, Woojin. 2017. "The Nature of Regional Voting and Its Change: Theoretical Issues and Empirical Analyses." *Journal of Legislative Studies* 50(1): 82-111.

Mosler, Hannes. 2008. "Why were District Party Chapters in 21 14 Abolished." *Journal of Korean Politics* 17(2): 121-161.

Mounk, Yascha. 2018. *The People vs. Democracy: Why Our Freedom Is in Danger and How to Save It.* Harvard University Press.

Mudde, Cas. 2016a. "Europe's Populist Surge: A Long Time in the Making." *Foreign Affairs* 95(6): 25-30.

Mudde, Cas. 2016b. *On Extremism and Democracy in Europe.* New York, NY: Routledge.

Mutz, Diana C. 2006. *Hearing the Other Side: Deliberative versus Participatory democracy.* Cambridge, UK: Cambridge University Press.

Newton, Kenneth and Pippa Norris. 2000. "Confidence in Public Institutions: Faith, Culture or Performance?", in S.J. Pharr and R. D. Putnam (eds.), *Disaffected Democracies: What's Troubling the Trilateral Countries?.* Princeton, NJ: Princeton University Press, pp. 52-73.

Nickerson, Raymond S. 1998. "Confirmation bias: A ubiquitous phenomenon in many guises." *Review of General Psychology* 2(2): 175-220.

Nunn, Clyde A., Harry J. Crockett, and Allen J. Williams. 1978. *Tolerance for Nonconformity.* San Francisco: Jossey-Bass.

Nyabola, Nanjala. 2018. *Digital Democracy, Analogue Politics: How the Internet Era is Transforming Kenya.* London: Zed Books

Oh, Dayyoung. 2018. "Learning Effects of Political Video Use in YouTube on Political Socialization: Focusing on Political Efficacy, Interest and Participation." *Journal of Education & Culture* 24(1): 97-115.

Papacharissi, Zizi. 2015. "We have always been social." *Social Media & Society* 1.

Retrieved from http://doi.org/10.11772056305115581185

Pariser, Eli. 2011. *The filter bubble: What the Internet is hiding from you.* New York: Penguin Press.

Park, Hun Myoung, and James L. Perry. 2008. "Do campaign web sites really matter in electoral civic engagement? Empirical evidence from the 2004 post-election Internet tracking survey." *Social Science Computer Review* 26: 190-212.

Park, Jae-Heung. 2001. "Theoretical and Methodological Issues in the Study of Generations." *Korea Journal of Population Studies* 24(2): 47-78.

Park, Jeeyoung and Jongbin Yoon. 2019. "The Crisis of Representative Democracy and Korean Platform Party in the Digital Age]." *Journal of Future Politics* 9(1): 119-142.

Park, Kyungmee and Jeon, Jin Young. 2019. "Party Leaders and Intra-party Democracy: Saenuri Party and Democratic United Party in the 19th National Assembly." *Journal of Parliamentary Research* 14(1): 47-71.

Park, Kyungmee. 2006. "Continuities and Changes of Party Organizations in Korea." The Doctoral Dissertation in Ewha Womens University.

Park, Kyungmee. 2010a. "Party Mergers and Splits in New Democracies: The Case of South Korea (1987-2007)." *Government and Opposition* 45(4), 531-552.

Park, Kyungmee. 2010b. "Party Switching of the First Republic: The Formation of the Liberal Party and the Democratic Party." Korean Party Studies Review 9(1): 5-37.

Park, Robert E., Ernest W. Burgess, and Roderick Duncan McKenzie. 1925. *The City.* Chicago: University of Chicago Press.

Park, Sang Soo. & Woon Seok Suh. 2012. "An Analysis of Social Inequality Cognition among Korea, China, and Japan." *Korean-Chinese Social Science Studies* 25(0), 104-128.

Park, Won Ho and Song Jung Min. 2012. "Do Parties Still Matter?: Independent Voters in Korean Elections." *Korean Politics Review* 21(2): 115-143.

Pasquale, Frank. 2015. *The black box society: The secret algorithms that control money and information.* New York: Harvard University Press.

Pateman, Carole. 2012. "Participatory Democracy Revisited." *Perspectives on Politics* 10(1): 7-19.

Pettigrew, Thomas F. 1998. "Intergroup Contact Theory." *Annual Review of Psychology* 49(1): 65-85.

Pettigrew, Thomas F., and Linda R. Tropp. 2006. "A Meta-Analytic Test of Intergroup Contact Theory." *Journal of Personality and Social Psychology* 90(5): 751-783.

Petty, Richard E., and John T. Cacioppo. 1986. *Communication and Persuasion: Central and Peripheral Routes to Attitude Change.* New York: Springer-Verlag.

Piketty, Thomas. 2014. *Capital in the Twenty-First Century.* Cambridge Massachusetts: The Belknap Press of Harvard University Press.

Pitkin, Hanna Fenichel. 1967. *The Concept of Representation.* Berkeley: University of California Press.

Portes, Alejandro, Patricia Fernandez-Kelly, and William Haller. 2005. "Segmented Assimilation on the Ground: The New Second Generation in Early Adulthood." *Ethnic and Racial Studies* 28(6): 1000-1040.

Prabhu, Devika. 2016. "Application of web 2.0 and web 3.0: An overview." *International Journal of Research in Library Science* 2: 54-62.

Prato, Carlo and Bruno Strulovici. 2017. "The hidden cost of direct democracy: How ballot initiatives affect politicians' Selection and incentives." *Journal of Theoretical Politics* 29(3): 440-466.

Prendergast, David. 2019. "The Judicial Role in Protecting Democracy from Populism." *German Law Journal* 20: 245-262.

Przeworski, Adam. 2019. *Crises of Democracy.* Cambridge: Cambridge University Press.

Qvortrup, Matt. ed. 2014. *Referendums around the world: The Continued Growth of Direct Democracy.* New York, NY: Palgrave Macmillan.

Rheingold, H. (2002). Smart Mobs: The Next Social Revolution. Cambridge: Perseus.

Robert J. Lavidge and Gary A. Steiner. 1961. "A Model for Predictive Measurements of Advertising Effectiveness." *Journal of Marketing* 25(6): 59-62.

Roberts, Nancy. 2004. "Public Deliberation in an Age of Direct Citizen Participation." *American Review of Public Administration* 34(4): 315-353.

Robertson, R. (1992). Globalization. London: Sage.

Röder, Antje, and Peter Mühlau. 2011. "Discrimination, Exclusion and Immigrants' Confidence in Public Institutions in Europe." *European Societies* 13(4): 535-557.

Safi, Mirna. 2010. "Immigrants' Life Satisfaction in Europe: Between Assimilation and Discrimination." *European Sociological Review* 26 (2): 159-176.

Samuel, Arthur L. 1967. "Some studies in machine learning using the game of checkers. II—Recent progress." *IBM Journal of research and development* 11(6): 601-617.

Schafer, J. Ben, Joseph A. Konstan, and John Riedl. 2001. "E-commerce recommendation applications." *Data mining and knowledge discovery* 5(1-2): 115-153.

Schedl, Markus, Zamani, Hamed, Chen, Ching-Wei, Deldjoo, Yashar, and Elahi, Mehdi. 2018. "Current challenges and visions in music recommender systems research." *International Journal of Multimedia Information Retrieval* 7(2): 95-116.

Schfer, Chelsea E. and Greg M. Shaw. 2009. "The Polls-Trends: Tolerance in the United States." *Public Opinion Quarterly* 73: 404-31.

Schildkraut, D. 2005. "The Rise and Fall of Political Engagement among Latinos: The Role of Identity and Perceptions of Discrimination." *Political Behavior* 27: 285-312.

Schmitt, Carl. 2008. *Constitutional Theory. Durham*. NC: Duke University Press.

Schmitter, Philippe C., and Terry Lynn Karl. 1991. "What Democracy Is … and Is Not." *Journal of Democracy* 2(3): 75-88.

Schradie, Jen. 2019. *The Revolution That Wasn't*. Cambridge, MA: Harvard University Press.

Schwab, K. (2016). The fourth industrial revolution. New York, NY: Crown Business.

Sears, David O. 1993. "Symbolic Politics: A Socio-psychological Theory," In Iyengar,S.,and McGuire, W. (eds.) *Explorations in Political Psychology* (pp.113-49). Durham, N.C:Duke University Press.

Seifert, Franz. 2006. "Local Steps in an International Career: a Danish-style Consensus Conference in Austria." *Public Understanding of Science* 15(1): 73-88.

Seo, Hyun-Jin. 2016. "Party Support and Political Trust in Korean National Assembly." *Dispute Resolution Studies Review* 14(2): 159-184.

Shin, Kwang-Yeong. 2012. "Economic Crisis, Neoliberal Reforms, and the Rise of

Precarious Work in South Korea." *American Behavioral Scientist* 57(3): 335-353.

Shortall, Sally. 2004. "Social or Economic Goals, Civic Inclusion or Exclusion? An Analysis of Rural Development Theory and Practice." *Sociologia Ruralis* 44(1): 109-123.

Slater, Dan. 2013. "Democratic careening." *World Politics* 65: 729-763.

Smith, Anthony D. 1991. *National Identity*. Reno: University of Nevada Press.

Smith, Graham and Corinne Wales. 2000. "Citizens' Juries and Deliberative Democracy." *Political Studies* 48: 51-65.

Smith, R. A., Smith, R., & Haider-Markel, D. P. (2002). Gay and lesbian Americans and political participation: A reference handbook. ABC-CLIO.

Sohn, Byoung Kwon et al. 2019. "The Analysis of the Causes of Generational Conflict." *Dispute Resolution Studies Review* 17(2): 5-37.

Solove, Daniel J. 2004. *The Digital Person: Technology and Privacy in the Information Age (Vol. 1)*. New York: NYU Press.

Somer, Murat, and Jennifer McCoy. 2018. "Dejá vu? Polarization and Endangered Democracies in the 21st Century." *American Behavioral Scientist* 62(1): 3-15.

Son, Nakgu. 2010. *Korean Political and Social Map: Metropolitan Area*. Seoul, Humanitas.

Song, Saem and Jae-Mook Lee. 2019. "The Analysis of Perception of Perennial Countries on Korean Peninsula by Generation: A Study on the Possibility of the overlap between South-South conflict and generation conflict." *Locality and Globality* 43(1): 117-141.

Statistics Korea. 2019. Population Census (2018). http://kosis.kr/statHtml/statHtml. do?orgId=101&tblId=DT_1JD1505&conn_path=I2

Staton, Jeffrey K., Christopher Reenock, Jordan Holsinger and Stafan Lindberg. "Can Courts be Bulwarks of Democracy?" V-Dem Working Paper 2018:71.

Stavrakakis, Yannis. 2018. "Paradoxes of Polarization: Democracy's Inherent Division and the (Anti-) Populist Challenge." *American Behavioral Scientist* 62(1): 43-58.

Stiglitz, Joseph E. 2012. *The Price of Inequality*. New York, NY: W.W. Norton & Company, Inc.

Storud, N. J. 2010. Polarization and partisan selective exposure. Journal of Communication 60, 556-576.

Stouffer, Samuel Andrew. 1955. *Communism, Conformity, and Civil Liberties: A Cross-Section of the Nation Speaks its Mind*. New Brunswick, New Jersey: Transaction Publishers.

Stouffer, Samuel C. 1955. *Communism, Conformity, and Civil Liberties*. New York: Doubleday.

Sullivan, John L. and Henriet Hendriks. 2009. "Public Support for Civil Liberties Pre- and Post-9/11." *Annual Review of Law and Social Sciences* 5: 375-91.

Sullivan, John L., James Piereson, and George E. Marcus. 1979. "An alternative conceptualization of political tolerance: Illusory increases 1950s-1970s." *American Political Science Review* 73(3): 781-794.

Sunstein, C. R. (2009). Neither Hayek nor Habermas. Public Choice, 124, 87-95.

Sunstein, Cass R. 2001. *Republic.Com*. Princeton: Princeton University Press.

Sweeney, Latanya. 2013. "Discrimination in online ad delivery." *Queue* 11(3): 10-29.

Tajfel, Henri. 1981. *Human Groups and Social Categories*. Cambridge: Cambridge University Press.

Tajfel, Henry and John C. Turner. 1986. "The Social Identity Theory of Intergroup Behavior". In. WORSHEL, S. and AUSTIN, W(eds.). *The Psychology of Intergroup Relations*. Chicago: Nelson-Hall.

The Public Deliberation Committee on Shin-Gori Nuclear Reactors No. 5 & 6. 2017. *Results of Participatory Surveys for Public Deliberation on. Shin-Gori Nuclear Reactors No. 5 & 6*.

Therborn, G. 2007. "Expert Group Meeting on Creating an Inclusive Society: Practical Strategies to Promote Social Integration." Presentation, Paris, France, 10 - 13 September 2007.

Tierney, Stephen. 2012. *Constitutional Referendums: The Theory and Practice of Republican Deliberation*. Oxford: Oxford University Press.

Tong, S. T., Heide, B., Langwell, L., & Walther, J. B. (2008). Too much of a good thing? The relationship between number of friends and interpersonal impressions on Facebook. Journal of Computer-Mediated Communication, 13, 531-549.

Turner, John C. 1999. "Some Current Issues in Research on Social Identity and Self-Categorization Theories". *Social identity: Context, Commitment, Content*: 6-34.

Tyler, Tom R. 2006. *Why People Obey the Law*. Princeton, NJ: Princeton University Press.

Voci, Alberto, and Miles Hewstone. 2003. "Intergroup contact and prejudice toward immigrants in Italy: The mediational role of anxiety and the moderational role of group salience." *Group Processes & Intergroup Relations* 6(1): 37-54.

Waldron, Jeremy. 1998. "Judicial Review and the Conditions of Democracy." *The Journal of Political Philosophy* 6(4): 335-355.

Waldron, Jeremy. 2006. "The core of the case against judicial review." *Yale Law Journal* 115(6): 1346.

Walker, A., & Wigfield, A. 2004. "The Social Inclusion Component of Social Quality." Working Paper.

Walker, Mark Clarence. 2003. *The Strategic Use of Referendums: Power, Legitimacy, and Democracy*. New York, NY: Palgrave Macmillan.

Wang, S. S., Moon, S-I., Kwon, K. H., Evans, C. A., & Stefanone, M. A. (2010). Face-off: Implications of visual cues on initiating friendship on Facebook. Computers in Human Behavior, 26, 226-234.

Waters, Mary C. 1999. *Black Identities: West Indian Immigrant Dreams and American Realities*. New York: Russell Sage Foundation.

Weber, Lori. 2003. "Rugged individuals and social butterflies: the consequences of social and individual political participation for political tolerance." *The Social Science Journal* 40(2): 335-342.

Wilson R. E., Gosling, S. D., & Graham, L. T. (2012). A review of Facebook research in the social sciences. Psychological Science 7, 203 -220.

Won, Sook-Yeon. 2014. "Social tolerance for foreigners and homosexuality and its policy implications: An exploratory study." *Korean Public Administration Review* 51(3): 225-256.

World Population Review. 2020. Most Diverse Countries 2020. http:// worldpopulationreview.com/countries/most-diverse-countries/

Yeo, Jun-suk. 2019. "Smart speaker privacy concerns spread to Korea." *The Korea Harold*. Retrieved from http://www.koreaherald.com/view.php?ud=201909090 008 80.

Yoo, Sung-jin, Jongbin Yoon, Sangjoon Ka, and Jinman Cho. 2011. "An Empirical

Analysis of Political Tolerance in Korea: Public Attitude toward Socio-political Rights of the Leat-liked Group." *National Strategy* 17(2): 69-90.

Yoo, Sung-jin. 2019. "Political Change and Tolerance: Social Security, Individual Orientation, and Democracy." *Dispute Resolution Studies Review* 17(3): 35-63.

Yoon, In-Jin and Youngho Song. 2011. "South Korean's Perceptions of National Identity and Acceptance of Multiculturalism." *The Korean Journal of Unification Affairs* 23(1), 143-192.

Yoon, Jong Bin, Kim Jin Ju and Jeong Hoi Ok. 2016. "An Analysis of Characteristics and Voting Behavior of Korean Political Independents: Focused on the 18th Presidential Election." *Institute for Humanities and Social Science* 17(1): 83-109.

Yoon, Jongbin, Jinman Cho, Sangjoon Ka, and Sungjin Yoo. 2011. "Tolerance Level and Disliked Groups in Korea." *The Korean Journal of Area Studied* 29(3): 161-185.

Yun, Seong Yi. 2012. *SNS & the Future of Participatory Democracy.* Nanam

Yun, Seong Yi and MinKyu Rhee. 2014. "Ideological conflict in young and older generations: Differences in ideology determinants and ideology representation." *21st Century Political Science Review* 24(3): 271-292.

Yun, Sun-Jin. 2005. "A Study on a Way of Public Participating Energy Governance: Based on an Evaluation of the Citizens' Consensus Conference on Electricity Policies in Korea." *Korean Society and Public Administration* 15(4): 121-153.

Zhang, Yin, and Louis Leung. 2015. "A review of social networking service (SNS) research in communication journals from 2006 to 2011." *New Media & Society* 17(7):1007-1024.

Zurn, Christopher F. 2002. "Deliberative Democracy and Constitutional Review." *Law and Philosophy* 21(4/5): 467-542.

Websites

ECOS(Economic Statistic System of Bank of Korea) http://ecos.bok.or.kr/

Kyunghyang-sinmun. 1947/06/11. "the Numbers of Parties and Social Groups Enrolled in the Public Opinion Department of American Military Government." From the National Institute of Korean History Digitalization of Korean History (http://www.history.go.kr).

OECD Data https://data.oecd.org/inequality/income-inequality.htm

OECD (2020), Income inequality indicator. (doi: 10.1787/459aa7f1-en (Accessed on 14 February 2020))

Reuter Institute Digital News Report (2019). [Available at https://reutersinstitute. politics.ox.ac.uk /sites/default/files/inline-files/DNR_2019_FINAL.pdf]

Social Survey Series of Statistics Korea (http://kostat.go.kr/portal/eng/index.action)

Statistics Korea http://kostat.go.kr/portal/eng/index.action

The Central Election Management Committee of Korea (www.nec.go.kr).

Jong Bin Yoon (Ph.D., University of Missouri, Columbia) is a director of Center for Future Policy Studies & a full professor in the Department of Political Science and Diplomacy at Myongji University, Republic of Korea. His research interests are electoral process, political parties, legislative behavior and theories of democracy.

Soo Hyun Jung (Ph.D., Florida State University) is a research professor in the Center for Future Policy Studies at Myongji University, Republic of Korea. His research interests are voting behavior, party politics, populism, regulatory enforcement and environmental politics.

Jeeyoung Park (Ph.D., State University of New York, Stony Brook) is a research professor in the Center for Future Policy Studies at Myongji University, Republic of Korea. Her research interests are voting behavior, public opinion, immigration, and political psychology.

Dong-Joon Jung (Ph. D., University of Florida) is Assistant Professor of social studies education at Inha University, Republic of Korea. With a regional focus on postcommunist Europe and South Korea, his research interests center upon democratization and regime transitions, comparative political behavior, parties and elections, civil society, gender and political attitudes.

Jungsub Shin (Ph.D., University of Missouri-Columbia) is an assistant professor in the Department of Political Science and International Relations at Soongsil University, Seoul, Republic of Korea. His main research interest lies in the area of comparative politics, with a focus on elections, political parties, and political economy.

Hoiok Jeong (Ph.D., University of Iowa) is an associate professor in the Department of Political Science at Myongji University, Republic of Korea. Her research interests are in minority politics, elections, religion and politics, and American politics.

Euisuok Han (Ph. D., University of Southern California) is an assistant professor in the Department of Political Science and Diplomacy, and the director of the Center for East Asian Studies at Sungshin Women's University, Seoul, Korea. His research interests include Japanese party politics and political economy.

Sung-jin Yoo (Ph.D., State University of New York at Stony Brook) is an associate professor of Scranton Honors Program, Ewha Womans University, Republic of Korea. His research interests are political behavior, political psychology, and public opinion.

Jinju Kim (Ph.D., Myongji University) is a research professor in the Center for Future Policy Studies at Myongji University, Republic of Korea. Her research interests are voting behavior, political parties, partisanship and multicultural politics.

Hana Kim (Ph.D., University of Georgia) is an associate professor in School of Communication at Dankook University, Republic of Korea. Her research interests are in effectiveness of persuasive message, especially political one, via traditional and new media based on psychology and consumer behavior.

Shin-Il Moon (Ph.D, University at Buffalo, The State University of New York) is an associate professor in the Department of Digital Media at Myongji University, Republic of Korea. His research interests are in the application of communication and social psychology theories in the areas of political, organizational, and new communication technology.

Kitae Kim (Ph.D, University at Buffalo, The State University of New York) is a research professor in the Center for Future Policy Studies at Myongji University, Republic of Korea. His research interests are in the application of communication and social psychology theories in the areas of health, organizational, and new communication technology.

Kyungmee Park (Ph.D., Ewha Womans University) is an associate professor in the Department of Political Science and Diplomacy at Jeonbuk National University, Republic of Korea. Her research interests are party politics, legislative politics, electoral politics and Korean politics.

Democracy and Social Change in South Korea

First Edition June 30, 2020
   reprinted in December 14, 2021
Author Jong Bin Yoon and Soo Hyun Jung et al.
Editor Center for Future Policy Studies
Publisher Seon-ki Kim
Published by Purengil. co., Ltd
Registration Number 16-1292
#1008 Daerung Post Tower 7. 48, Digital-ro 33gil, Guro-gu, Seoul, Republic of Korea
E-mail purungilbook@naver.com
Homepage http://www.purungil.co.kr
Phone +82-2-523-2907
Fax +82-2-523-2951

Printed in Korea
ISBN 978-89-6291-871-7 93340

This work was supported by the Ministry of Education of the Republic of Korea and the National Research Foundation of Korea. (NRF-2019S1A3A2098969)